DEGROWTH

An Experience of Being Finite

Pasi Heikkurinen

Published by Mayfly Books. Available in paperback
and free online at www.mayflybooks.org in 2024.

ISBN (Print)   978-1-906948-72-6
ISBN (PDF)   978-1-906948-73-3

Images © 2024 Jani Anders Purhonen

may f l y

This book is dedicated to

Fjalar Ukko and Viena Edla
(and other kids vigorously engaging in limits testing)

Contents

Publisher's foreword

MayFly Books is a radical and subversive open-access micro-printing press, an outlet for scholars, run by scholars, for the people. We aim to publish books that matter and provide content that we endorse, support, and defend. From the very beginning, our aim has been to challenge the system, and by this we not only mean challenging the academic publishing mafia but refer more broadly to challenging the unsustainable and unjust capitalist system.

Pasi Heikkurinen's *Degrowth: An Experience of Being Finite* is the perfect follow-up to MayFly's previous volumes related to degrowth. In the book the author argues that degrowth is first and foremost an experience and only secondarily an anti-capitalist idea, a research field, and the degrowth movement. It is this experience that underlies—or grants us access to—all anti-capitalist initiatives and acts leading to the degrowth of the physical size of the economy. We are only able to purposefully slow down, redistribute, and take care of the present and future generations of life by experiencing degrowth. The experience of degrowth is about learning to inhabit a finite world together with others. To succeed in this—and as Heikkurinen convincingly argues—we who overshoot must re-examine *being, technology, transformation, culture,* and *nature* in relation to ourselves. The author proposes that the degrowth movement defines limits from within and keeps itself within those limits in order to transition from the Great Acceleration (defined by fossil-technological hubris).

While it is true that the literature on degrowth is currently blossoming—well over 1000 peer-reviewed articles on degrowth have been published within 15 years—the phenomenological approach to degrowth that Heikkurinen offers in this book has remained missing until today. *Degrowth: An Experience of Being Finite* is a focal contribution to this field of discovery, particularly as it challenges us to make sense of degrowth and our worldly finiteness through our personal experience as embodied beings, embedded in the greater constellation of life.

I have known the author for well over ten years and published over 25 different texts with him within the past decade. However, our collaboration has not (yet) extended to the field of degrowth, which was one of the reasons why I was happy to accept his book proposal and publish the book through MayFly Books. The book publication project started as a collection of previously published articles but ended up as a carefully re-written theorization of degrowth and the experience of finitude. It is a key text because it not only confronts the current insatiable capitalist growth economy, but also pushes forward, challenging the hegemony of science and technology. While doing so, Heikkurinen asks us to embark on a journey of personal and communal metamorphosis. On this voyage we are asked to *let go of*, or to *release*, the nature-/self-destroying will to transform. The author calls for a sort of anti-transformational being that restores balance by letting things be and allowing them to recover without human intervention. For Heikkurinen, degrowth is surely not another Green New Deal or ecological reconstruction project, it is a process of coming to terms with the boundaries and limits of human doings.

Compared with many degrowth contributions, the style and tone of the book is exquisitely reflexive. However, it manages to eloquently move from its philosophical remarks to practical implications. The book is deeply theoretical and philosophical, which is a refreshing wind, breathing life into the discussions on degrowth, including the emerging debate on degrowth communism. Whilst reading the book, the reader should grasp why degrowth theory is so important for the degrowth movement. We are clearly dealing with big questions and topics, so perhaps we should stop and think more! After all, degrowth is still a relatively young field of inquiry that has plenty to say about the wrongs in the world, but it has not yet truly tackled the issues that Heikkurinen places on the table, including the seemingly insatiable human drive to produce and transform nature ever more.

To advance the degrowth movement, we need both critical research and more reflexive, philosophical enquiries—like those found in this book. As Heikkurinen reminds us, all this must be accompanied by our collective metamorphosis into peaceful coexistence. The experience of being finite is fundamental for this change to happen.

Toni Ruuska
Co-editor of MayFly Books

Acknowledgements

There are numerous people deserving thanks for the emergence of this book. First, I must express my deepest gratitude to my longest-standing and closest colleague, Dr Toni Ruuska. We have been working together on degrowth-related questions for over a decade now. We have written a lot but also done some sombre activist stuff. As colleagues, we have also attempted to see other people with rather poor results. Luckily, there is some light at the end of the tunnel—which brings me to thanking the brilliant scholars in our research group, Process Studies on Sustainable Economy (helsinki.fi/prose). I must give kudos to Dr Jarkko Pyysiäinen, the current director of the group, and Dr Campbell Jones, the most recent affiliate who kindly offered invaluable comments on this book manuscript. It is a great privilege to be able to converse and collaborate with you. Thank you tremendously!

I am also deeply indebted to the group's younger generation of scholars for their energy and inspiration (they are listed alphabetically by their last names): Johanna Hohenthal, Eeva Houtbeckers, Joshua Hurtado Hurtado, Jessica Jungell-Michelsson, Tommi Kauppinen, Tina Nyfors, Heini A. Salonen, Milla Suomalainen, and Joonas Uotinen. And now that the youth/elderly axis is introduced, I will move to the other end of the continuum to thank my timeworn mentor who keeps supporting me, Dr Karl Johan Bonnedahl. Your analytical skills and humour combined with sincere care continues to be a central signpost for me. Since it was you with whom I founded the Sustainable Change Research Network (suchresearch.net), we can smoothly transition onto acknowledging all the people in this international collective. Thank you all for your engagement!

In addition to recognizing my co-authors for my degrowth-related publications (listed alphabetically by their first names)Anna Kuokkanen, Anu Valtonen, Ashly Pinnington, Ben Robra, David Skrbina, Elena Hofferberth, Elizabeth Morgan, Iana Nesterova, Jana Lozanoska, Jenny Rinkinen, Jose Manuel Alcaraz, Jouni Paavola, Juha Helenius, Jukka Hoffrén, Jukka Mäkinen, Kari Koppelmäki, Katerina Nicolopoulou, Konsta Nylander, Kristoffer Wilén, Marko Ulvila, Outi Rantala, Pasi Takkinen, Pierre Tosi, Sally Russell, Sanna Ahvenharju, Sophia Hagolani-Albov, Stewart Clegg, Stefan Gold, Timo Järvensivu, Todd LeVasseur, Tommi Lehtonen, Vilma Hämäläinen, and William C. Young—I wish to thank my colleagues related to the (international) Degrowth Movement (listed alphabetically by their first names): Adrián Almazán, Aleksander Žolja, Amos Wallgren, Andreas Roos, Beth Strathford, Christian Kerschner, Dan O'Neill, Elgars Felcis, Elke Pirgmaier, Erik Swyngedouw, Federico Demaria, Giacomo D'Alisa, Giorgios Kallis, Isabelle Guillon, Jess Parker, Joachim Spangenberg, Julia Steinberger, Karen Bakker, Linda Nierling, Logan Strenchock, Martin Fritz, Max Koch, Melf-Hinrich Ehlers, Milena Büchs, Niklas Toivakainen, Petra Wächter, Rakel Similä, Robson Rocha, Sylvia Lorek, Tamas Veress, Teemu Vaarakallio, Teppo Eskelinen, Thomas Wallgren, Tuuli Hirvilammi, and Laua Wiman. Thank you for your interest, conviviality, and support.

And before thanking my partner, I would like to acknowledge all my friends who are keen on, or have sympathy (and more!) for, the degrowth cause, including (in random order) Eeva-Stiina and Paula Lönnemö, Risto Musta, Jussi Sivenius, Mikko Jalas, Torsti Hyyryläinen, Lasse Nordlund and Maria Dorff, Isabelle Guillon, Justine Bernachon-Irisarri, Simo Häkli, Tanja Niiranen, Pekka

Mehtonen, Jani A. Purhonen, Tere Vadén, and Eeva Rönkä. For
the most recent intellectual stimuli, I wish to thank Pauli Pylkkö,
Tim Ingold, Ariel Salleh, Niilo Kauppi, Thomas Princen, Wendelin
Küpers, and Arran Gare. Your thought and writings have kept me
going. Finally, and most importantly, thank you Jenny for your
care and love. You and the kids mean the (life)world to me!

This work was supported by the Research Council of Finland
(grant number 343277).

Introduction

We are told that since the Industrial Revolution (from the eighteenth century onwards), the ecosphere[1], including its local ecosystems, has undergone drastic changes in terms of rising temperatures and habitat destruction (see, e.g. Zalasiewicz et al., 2008; Barnosky et al., 2012). Some of us have witnessed these changes in person. The so-called species extinction debt is found to begin to cumulate at the advent of the Second Industrial Revolution (Liao et al., 2022; see also Figueiredo et al., 2019). This era, which took place from the late nineteenth century into the early twentieth century, is better known as the Technological Revolution. According to the IPCC (2014; 2023), the principal causes of global warming are anthropogenic greenhouse gas emissions, which in turn are the undesired outcomes of the still ongoing economic and population growth (see also Dietz and Rosa, 1997; UNEP, 2011; Lorek and Spangenberg, 2014).

The growth of the human sphere has meant increasing demands for food, mobility, housing, and other goods and services (cf. Latouche, [2007] 2009; Jackson, 2009). The production for the mounting needs and wants has led not only to growing pressure on the atmosphere through emissions but also to greater damage on land and water, signifying habitats being exploited for production

---

1 Ecosphere refers to the global sum of Earth's ecosystems comprising of both biotic (living) and abiotic (not living) entities. The etymology of *eco-* is from Greek *oîkos* (οἶκος) referring to 'family' and 'house', while *sphere* comes from the word *sphaira* (σφαῖρα) denoting 'ball'. Apart from solar and cosmic radiation entering and exiting the planet, the ecosphere is a relatively closed system.

purposes (Barnosky et al., 2012). During the period of fierce technological advancement, '[a]nnual global resource extraction and use increased from about 7 billion tons (7 Gt) in 1900 to about 55 billion tons (55 Gt) in 2000, with the main shift being from renewable biotic resources to non-renewable mineral ones' (UNEP, 2011, p. 17; see also Oberle et al., 2019).

The expansion of human activities has also signified the transformation of the terrestrial biosphere into so-called anthromes (Ellis, 2011) or human-made objects 'passing the 50% mark early in the 20th century' (Ellis et al., 2010). For example, 'about 40% of all ice-free land on Earth is in direct use for agriculture or urban settlements' and '[a]n additional 37% of ice-free land is not currently used for these purposes but is embedded within anthromes having these uses' (Ellis et al., 2010, p. 603). Another way to put this is to refer to the present crossover point, where the human-made or anthropogenic mass, doubling roughly every 20 years, surpasses the living biomass (Elhacham et al., 2020). Hence—despite some advances in the health of selected humans and local ecosystems—it is rather apparent that the consequences of techno-capitalist production have been global and detrimental for earthbound beings.

This kind of growth has been empowered by the advances in technology and the utilization of natural resources (Hornborg, 2014), particularly fossil energy (Malm, 2016; see also Wrigley, 2010). The development, however, is now being confronted as ecosystems are setting limits to the expansion of human activity (Rockström et al., 2009; Steffen et al., 2015; Richardson et al., 2023). As regards material limits, stocks of non-renewable natural resources are heading towards depletion, and renewable resources (such as forests and stocks of fish) are being consumed faster than they can renew themselves (Daly, 1996; Lorek and Spangenberg, 2014). Similar patterns can be found in the human psyche as the ecology of mind can also be over-burdened (Heikkurinen et al., 2019a). Regarding the less tangible limits in non-human nature, the atmospheric carbon dioxide concentration has been found to be too great and the global nitrogen cycle too disrupted to ensure a safe operating space for humanity and other species (Rockström et al., 2009; Steffen et al., 2015; Richardson et al., 2023). These estimates concerning the state of the ecosphere are certainly beset by uncertainties, but the principal point holds: if humans are to steer away from the current worst-case scenario of collapsing ecosystems, our cultures, particularly the over-consuming and over-producing ones, must be radically reorganized (Goodland and Daly, 1996; also, Barnosky et al., 2012; Ritchie et al., 2021).

Well, we all sort of know this. Or at least we could say that only some of these facts are new to us. But then again, they probably do not change the big picture of the Technological Revolution radically worsening the state of ecospheric affairs. The grand narrative is about the radical changes in human–nature relata taking place around the period from the 1700–1900s. And this is also where the infamous hockey stick curve has its base. It is the same story that has been in public awareness at least since the Brundtland Commission (WCED, 1987) that reported on the problems of increasing affluence and an increasing population, as well as reporting on these problems beginning to cast a shadow on the role of technology (see Bonnedahl et al., 2022). Similar remarks on growth, albeit perhaps slightly gloomier ones, were made by the *Limits to Growth* (Meadows et al., 1972) reports. So why write another book on the problem of growth and the only feasible solution, the call to de-grow? Do we not all already know this? Should we not move directly beyond growth and engage in the positive psychology of the post-growth narrative? That is, should we not be less pessimistic and confrontative? Could we talk about something nice like sustainability or planetary well-being? Is not the term *degrowth* such an aggressive one? Should we let go of this *word grenade*, as Serge Latouche calls degrowth?

The short answer to rejecting the degrowth discourse is no. The destructive power of increased throughput[2]—particularly via

---

2 'An entropic process in the biosphere and a concept describing Earth's anthropogenic

mounting affluence—is unfortunately still not very well known. And even if it is known, it is not enacted upon. It seems like that an understanding of what degrowth signifies in experience is still largely missing. Also, the question concerning technology is too ambiguous. It goes without saying that we will eventually move to a beautiful time and place after growth, be it by disaster or design or something in between the two, but we can only go there by *degrowing*. In other words, there will be no agrowth, postgrowth, sustainability, or planetary well-being without degrowth, but there can be degrowth without the imaginaries of an after-growth era. Degrowth is a necessary condition for continuing diverse life on earth.

The postgrowth discourse, for instance, is surely needed, but it will be idle and empty, a projectionist fantasyland, unless accompanied by *degrowth*. There is a lot of (non-monetary) work to be done before we can leave growth behind or move beyond it. And lastly, degrowth as a term and movement are far from being aggressive and violent. If any term can be hostile and assertive, blood hungry, it is *growth*. The same applies to any discourses and narratives rejecting the necessity to degrow the human sphere in the ecosphere. Growth as a one-dimensional movement of the techno-capitalist system is a negation of life. Deprived of phases of degrowth, growth as an organizing principle for any culture is a recipe for decadence, death, and decay. A thriving culture has a lifecycle of growth, degrowth, and postgrowth—and now, it is time to degrow the over-affluent globe, societies, communities, households, and individuals.

This book is distinct from other books on degrowth in

---

metabolic flow. It refers to objects that travel through the human sphere, entering as (low-entropy) resources (or natural capital)—such as wood, coal, and precious metals—and exiting as (high-entropy) waste to air, land, and water. These objects are commonly defined as either "matter" and/or "energy," and thence the terms "matter-energetic throughput" and "material throughput" are used. If the analysis of the metabolic flow (input–output) is limited to an economic unit—for example, a firm, a household, or a national economy—then the term "economic throughput" is used. Owing to human embeddedness in nature, every human act (for example, a new product or service) requires matter-energy and alters the amount and quality of throughput. The greater the throughput, the greater the amount of high entropy.' (Heikkurinen, 2023, pp. 545–546).

that it approaches the topic from theoretical, conceptual and philosophical points of view. It will investigate degrowth as a phenomenon that manifests in various forms. And by doing so, the book encourages the reader to experiment with multiple interpretations of degrowth and ask what degrowth is and what it is not. Instead of treating degrowth from a single perspective with no or little further specifications, the book encourages readers to situate degrowth in a particular context and hereby draw boundaries around the phenomenon. For instance, when you say *degrowth* do you mean, for example the degrowth movement, the actual decrease in the human use of matter-energy or something else (like a discourse or a metaphor)? And further specifications will naturally follow as we delineate.

This book invites you to consider degrowth as an experience, something everyone can and will (co-)entre through lived experience sooner or later. I define *experiences* broadly as those things that (more or less) enter our consciousness and leave a mark, enabling us to meaningfully act in, as well as speculate about, the world. By the notion of them 'more or less entering' doing this I again want to underscore that not all experiences of degrowth are equally conscious—some remain more hidden. Furthermore, the book's definition of *experience* is not limited to (embodied) humans but includes all beings' capability to experience degrowth. The approach developed is phenomenological, perhaps anti-positivist, and I guess you could also call it a negativist one. It is perchance gloomy by being inclusive towards darkness and despair. When it comes to the techno-capitalist system, at least the undercurrent of the book is culturally pessimistic. There simply is no light at the end of that tunnel. We must leave the tunnel.

In addition to being indebted to Edmund Husserl and Maurice Merleau-Ponty for their work on what experience is and also being indebted to Arne Naess and Georg Henrik von Wright for their work on human cultures' place in nature, I will approach degrowth as an experience (of being finite) with the help of Martin Heidegger, Friedrich Nietzsche, and Alfred North Whitehead. Of course, I will also engage with my contemporaries and the (deep) evergreen concerns of the degrowth movement. These questions are about technology, change, and nature, in particular: how could technology assist us in the movement, how can one contribute to effective change, and how can one talk about nature... or is everything cultural now? To answer these questions, my paramount influence from within the degrowth movement comes from Nicholas Georgescu-Roegen and Serge Latouche.

The book consists of 50 focal issues of contemporary degrowth theory, structured around seven chapters. The first chapter[3] is titled 'Enframing' and it argues that technology will not be useful for the degrowth movement's ambition to reduce matter-energy throughput. Every engagement in and with technological practices requires matter-energy, hereby adding to the cumulative anthropogenic mass. There are surely differences in technological practices. These are conceptualised as degrees of technology. The practice of swimming in shorts in a lake does not increase the matter-energy throughput as much as swimming in a scuba gear in a heated pool. It is also largely problematic if we detach a technological instrument or a technological practice from the rest of the techno-capitalist system. Even producing and consuming a single technological instrument, like a pair of swim trunks, contributes to growth. The ethical implications for the degrowth movement to follow are refraining from technological practice by releasement; 'Releasement' is the title of Chapter 2. The new ethos of letting be signifies focusing on being, not on technologies. This allows the world and its beings to unfold their manifold genesis.

The third chapter[4] of this book is called 'Transformation'. It can be read as a commentary on the prevailing frenzy to quickly do

3 Chapters 1 and 2 were originally published in 2018 under the title 'Degrowth by means of technology? A treatise for an ethos of releasement' (197, pp. 1654–1665) in *Journal of Cleaner Production*, in a special issue entitled 'Degrowth and Technology: Towards feasible, viable, appropriate and convivial imaginaries', edited by Christian Kerschner, Petra Wächter, Linda Nierling, and Melf-Hinrich Ehlers. Republished with permission.
4 Chapters 3 and 4 are based on an article 'Degrowth: A metamorphosis in being', which was originally published in 2019 in *Environment and Planning E: Nature and Space*, 2(3),

something major. The chapter conceptualizes and problematizes the human so-called will-to-transform by showing a fundamental paradox in the discourse. On the one hand, the problem is the transformation of nature, which calls us to transform our culture so that it will not transform nature as much, but then, on the other hand, the manner in which transformations are done requires the further transformation of nature. A prime example of this are 'green' investment packages: energy use is found to be too high; thus, we need to change; but in order to change, we use more energy, which eventually does not reduce the overall energy use. The next chapter, 'Metamorphosis', suggests that instead of calling for further transformations, a change in being is needed. And this metamorphosis begins when we surrender to waiting— not awaiting—which is well ridiculed in Samuel Beckett's *Waiting for Godot*.

The book's fifth chapter,[5] titled 'Nature's Cultures', deals with the human place in the ecosphere. It addresses the seeming conflict of humans feeling alienation and estrangement from nature while being embedded in it. This riddle has led many scholars to either reproduce the human–nature dualism or let go of the concept of nature altogether. The chapter implies that the issue of whether humans should return to nature or not is a false-premise question. We humans can never return to nature because we never left it. But then, how can we explain the experience of estrangement or alienation? In Chapter 6, 'The Core of Nature', the book proceeds to suggests that there is no puzzlement about the human–nature relation if we assume that nature has a core. If there is a core of nature, that enables us to be estranged from the core of nature while still be part of nature. That is, it is plausible that many of us are (more or less) far from the core of nature, while still being part of

pp. 528–547, as part of the special issue 'Geographies of Degrowth', edited by Federico Demaria, Giorgos Kallis, and Karen Bakker. Republished with permission.
5 Chapters 4 and 5 are based on an original article (Heikkurinen, 2021) published in *Environmental Values* (30: 3, pp. 367–385) edited by Clive Spash. The title of the article is 'The nature of degrowth: Theorising the core of nature for the degrowth movement' and this work is republished with permission.

nature. The core is made intelligible by three temporal perspectives of which the first one is romantic and the second futurist. The chapter suggests that the degrowth movement should now emphasize present nature, not nature of the past or nature to come. This is the third perspective, it is about *being* in the present tense, not about living in some ideal projection or in the good old days.

The final chapter discusses five practical implications of the book's theorising for the degrowth movement. It demonstrates the following:

– how we can get more real with our smallest common denominator, namely the reduction of matter-energy throughput,

– how to better understand the metabolic base of our culture,

– how to reject the uprightly tempting goal of providing a good life for everyone, all the time, everywhere,

– how to experience limits directly,

– how a cosmic consideration could advance the degrowth movement

In addition to these implications, from the book's chapters on the three grand themes of technology (Chapters 1–2), change (Chapters 3–4), and nature (Chapters 5–6), I draw the main conclusion. The degrowth movement, including its scholarship, should pay more attention to *being*.[6] At its simplest, this means that we ought to explore, discuss and change (i.a.) the way we *are*. It is not enough to look at language, activities, or structures, more emphasis must

---

6 The book, while being largely indebted to Heidegger's *Being and Time* ([1927] 2012) in its conceptulization of being, always refers to *co-being* when talking about *being*, as advised by Nancy ([1996] 2000), and is not limited to treating *being* as merely '*being human*' but also encompassess non-humans in its understanding (see, e.g. Latour, [1999] 2009) and situates being in—or 'throws' being into—more-than-human worlds (Abram, 1996). In addition, being is never reduced to a mere relation, as suggested by Harman (2009).

be placed on *being degrowth*. The techno-capitalist system cannot be challenged by merely gaining the means of production or appropriating corrupt means for virtuous purposes. The growth imperative runs much deeper in our cultural fabric. It is in our mode of being, the way we are in the world.

A precondition for countering the increasing matter-energy throughput is to refrain from highly technological practices, as well as stop being single-mindedly about low tech. Change in the so-called ontic register is not enough. The degrowth movement must stress the register of the ontological. Every step down the technology ladder is surely claimed to be supportive of slowing down human–nature's metabolism. But *being* does not reduce to thermodynamic applications either. The will-to-transform simply cannot be directed to degrowth as it distracts us from *being*. The move from the growth mode of being to one of degrowth requires a metamorphosis. It is fundamental, nothing gradual, and it results in a completely different way of living, which could be called *dwelling*. It is not only a new ethic, not to mention a new policy, but also another aesthetic. The good and beautiful in the degrowth mode of being are built on the experience of finitude, a deep (embodied) understanding that everything has limits. Degrowth as the experience of finitude also signifies a new temporal understanding which spotlights 'the present'. We are neither no longer paralysed by sadness or driven by the anger related to the destroyed world, nor are we expecting the world to become something beautiful and good which revitalizes us. We dwell in the lifeworld into which we are thrown in.

Somewhat circularly, by caressing the experience of degrowth, we may be let in to realize the lessons and intricacies of the limits of being (i.e. the fact that being is finite). This is nothing metaphysical in the sense that there would be something like non-being (a sphere where things come into being), but that there are limits, nevertheless. Limits are nothing imposed on us by the natural sciences or policy makers; they are something that we should collectively fathom. And for us to be able to collectively deliberate, discuss, and determine the limits, we must experience the limits. In this way we will not be left at the vagaries of science and the continued misuse of power in the techno-capitalist system.

The focal premises of the book's argument originate in the ecological philosophies of experience or eco-phenomenology. The book assumes that we cannot access understandings of degrowth, or any other phenomenon embedded in nature, and the consequent question of what to do about it, outside our experience. It is experience which grants us an access to sagacity, allowing us to understand what it means to be in the world. Be it degrowth, post-growth, or growth, an experiential approach is indispensable. The book will thereof investigate its questions in close conceptual proximity to not only degrowth as experience but also with the overall leitmotif of the experience of being finite.

**

The book's overall argument is that degrowth requires experiencing the finitude of being or that degrowth necessitates the experience of being finite, as the title indicates. An act of degrowth is certainly possible without going deep in degrowth; consider, for example, a pop-up bike repair workshop with home-brewed beer and self-grown carrots. But maintaining the degrowth spirit across time and space with continued outcomes that are desirable in terms of matter-energy will necessitate a holistic existential turnaround: *being degrowth*.

This book—like so many, I assume—is largely born out of frustration. What troubles me is that so many people in my culture do not have a sense of limits. Every day we hear and read about misdemeanours of varying sorts. Too many people, too often, go too far by crossing boundaries. Most recently, of course, the war in Ukraine is example of this par excellence, but classics—like over-consumption and over-production or even hubris—are also fitting examples of our lack of understanding of the limits. Certainly not all people, not even in my sub-culture of rather Western over-educated white (mainly) heterosexual men, are uniformly out of touch with the restrictions of the world, be it reflected in the amount of politically incorrect jokes or the severity of titillating harassment. But luckily there are also skilled people—those who stay within the bounds. Nevertheless, it is the reckless action and discourses, and particularly the rejection of limits, which drove me compile this book.

While I call for the experience of limits; limiting ourselves and others (co-limiting) from within the movement—this also involves some limits testing. The act of testing limits, like kids often do, is necessary but should be done with care and caution. In fact, as long as limits are acknowledged and respected, such precautionary limits testing is not the major problem. Rather it is the immature assumption of infinity and the consequent absence of consideration for identifying and abiding to limits. Every thing must have limits. Otherwise, it would not be 'a thing'. A thing is that which is defined by its limits. Also, anything can go too far or lack something so, in that sense, things are also finite. The cosmos and nature, as well as our being in the world and our understanding of these, are limited. The technology we use (and the technology that uses us) is limited. AI, for instance, is also limited by being earthbound—nothing escapes the matter-energetic metabolism of the ecosphere. Ideas, thoughts, souls, and psyches are all bounded by our worldly affairs, including the flow of matter-energic exchanges between humans and nature.

The degrowth movement is a prominent promoter of limits, at least in Europe. On its webpage (degrowth.info), it 'advocates for societies that prioritize social and ecological well-being instead of corporate profits, over-production and excess consumption'. This cultural shift is claimed to necessitate 'radical redistribution, reduction in the material size of the global economy, and a shift in common values towards care, solidarity and autonomy. Degrowth means transforming societies to ensure environmental justice and a good life for all within planetary boundaries.' Pretty neat, right? Who could object to this?

My opening degrowth event was organized in Helsinki in 2010.

The speakers included Serge Latouche, Peter Victor, and Tim Jackson. I gathered I wanted to become part of the movement and participated in the International Degrowth Conferences in Budapest (2016), Malmö (2018), and Zagreb (2023). I have also been a moderately active member of the Finnish Degrowth Network (*Kohtuusliike*). But to my surprise, instead of seeking to gain a shared understanding on what and/or where the limits of our collective action are—not to mention exploring how to stay within them—the meetings have revolved around a rather general, universal ethical concern for all people and the planet. It seems that the boundaries are taken as given and treated rather as an impetus for action. It is as if the 'limits' were unnegotiable—a rigid policy for an affirmative consumption corridor in which all human action take place.

What also seems to go basically unquestioned within the degrowth movement, and in parallel with this structure of limits, is the role of natural sciences informing policy by providing the lower and upper thresholds for our enactments. However, with the help of social sciences and humanities, such a positivist practice should also be subjected to critical inquiry. It is not only the lack of epistemological scrupulousness that worries me but also the political naivety of the movement. Even if we knew how to demarcate definite boundaries between humans and nature (for instance, in the case of deciding when there are simply too many emissions or where the safe habitat destruction space actually is) the problems of power and mobilization will follow unresolved.

What I mean by this is that the numbers we in the degrowth movement use may not only legitimize inertia by reproducing the techno-capitalist culture of growth, they may also be used calculatedly against the interests of minority cultures and the needs of non-humans and the more-than human. How could we trust, let us say, that the relationship between the techno-capitalist scientist and the policymaker will be such that adequate and effective precautionary action will be legislated? Owing to the blood-stained history of scientific method, how could we expect that today's scientific knowledge on limits will not be misused (again) for the benefit of the elite? Do we see that limits defined by the scientific apparatus are mobilizing social movements in the right direction (read: moving towards being metabolically slower)?

Rather than answering these questions, this book will complement the discussion on limits with a take from within. By *within*, I do not mean anything greatly esoteric or spiritual, or even individualistic but rather refer to the precondition of the degrowth movement engaging in the (collective) processes of co-understanding what can and cannot be done. My frustration is thus partly also about seeing how the degrowth movement is increasingly becoming dependent on the knowledge-producing and consuming machine that is inherently linked to the techno-capitalist culture that is yielding growth. With the sub-title *An Experience of Being Finite*, I also want to open up a debate on the limits of the degrowth movement itself. Nothing is omnipotent, not even our dear movement. But in what respect are we limited?

The intention of the book's critique is, on the one hand, directed at those promoting the growth of affluence, population, and technology (i.e. the proponents of techno-capitalism) but, on the other hand, also those within the degrowth movement (i.e. the only imaginable alternative) who rely on science as their utmost authority for defining limits. I sincerely hope that this book will be an adequately compelling read and help the degrowth movement to *slow down and thereby gain momentum*. I also hope that the book will cause its readers to refrain from economically (more) productive activity and find finitude in being.

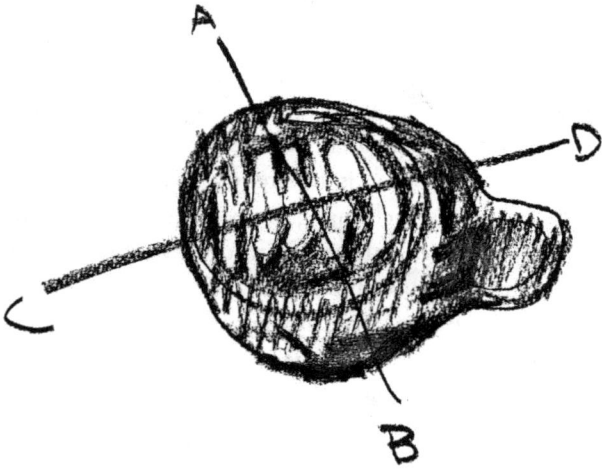

CHAPTER ONE
Enframing

This chapter claims that growth culture is largely defined by the technological mode of being. This so-called enframing is ecologically unsustainable and does not support the emergence of moral agency for social change that could reduce matter-energy throughput.

1. Ecomodernity

Modernity first mutated into post-modernism and now further mutated to eco-modernism. It is eco-modernists that are today too much in charge of steering cultural development. In their technocratic governance, advanced technical tools and instruments are combined with logic from selected natural sciences and engineering to form 'technology', the silver bullet for solving global and local ecological problems (UN, 2012; IPCC, 2014; 2023; EC, 2015). In line with suggestions made by ecological modernization theorists (e.g. Mol and Spaargaren, 2000; Mol and Sonnenfeld, 2000; Jänicke, 2008), vast amounts of time and energy are directed towards research, and the development and innovation of new, 'greener', or 'cleaner' products and processes. Measured in economic terms, global investments in the so-called clean energy, for instance, reached USD 318 billion in 2014 (BNEF, 2015). Once it reaches its fullest potential by directing sufficient capital to the brightest minds of the planet, it is believed that the New Technological Revolution will deliver solutions to the most challenging problems of our time.

2. Anti-decoupling

This all builds on the assumption of decoupling. Within the prevalent system of capitalism, where the accumulation of capital must never be jeopardized (Boltanski and Chiapello [1999] 2005; Latouche, [2007] 2009), solutions to the escalating ecospheric crisis have become narrowly defined as those that contribute to decoupling (Næss and Høyer, 2009). This fantasy of decoupling embeds an idea that further economic growth would not necessarily result in ecological harm if more advanced technology manifests rapidly enough.

There is, however, strong empirical and theoretical evidence of the correlation, as well as of the causality, of economic growth and ecological destruction (Næss, [1974] 1989; Daly, 1979, 1996; IPCC, 2014, 2023; Hickel and Kallis, 2020). It is broadly acknowledged in ecological economics that the expansion of economic activity signifies a greater use of natural resources and a greater volume of greenhouse gas emissions (e.g. Victor, 2008; Jackson, 2009; Hickel and Kallis, 2019). The success claimed to result from decoupling economic growth from ecological damage is based on selected data in terms of geographical context (see, e.g. Zhang, 2000; Tapio, 2005; de Freitas and Kaneko, 2011). The problem with such research designs is that the outsourced production (input) and exportation of waste (output) to other countries are excluded from the calculus. As demonstrated by Wiedmann et al. (2015), when examining decoupling with global material flow data, the reported achievement per country is considerably less than assumed and is even non-existent in some cases.

Due to the lack of robust evidence of absolute decoupling (Daly, 1996; Victor, 2008; Jackson, 2009; Hickel and Kallis, 2020; Parrique et al., 2019), there is a call for a transition from growth economies to degrowth societies in order to achieve sustainability (Martínez-Alier et al., 2010; Cattaneo et al., 2012; Sekulova et al., 2013; Kallis et al., 2012; D'Alisa et al., 2015). In this scenario, instead of building up expectations and furthering ungrounded optimism in technological progress, the economies of the world would be downsized to the extent that their resource use and waste do not exceed the regenerative and/or assimilative capacities of the planetary ecosystem (Daly, 1996; Dietz and O'Neill, 2013). Given the extremely inequitable distribution of wealth (Piketty, [2013] 2014) and the relatively small reduction potential in the Global South (UNEP, 2011), degrowth would have to begin in the wealthiest economies of the world (Georgescu-Roegen, 1975; Daly, 1996; Latouche, [2007] 2009) and comprise (human) affluence reductions (Bonnedahl and Heikkurinen, 2019).

This book conceptualizes, employs, and advances a so-called minimalistic definition of *degrowth*. This means that *degrowth* is first and foremost used to refer to the reduction of the size of an economy, which is measured in matter-energy throughput. This is the metabolic flow an economy. The degrowth movement, however, is not limited to the minimalist definition but encompasses a wider perspective on cultural change (see, e.g. Latouche, [2007] 2009).

Since degrowth signifies that 'societies will use fewer natural resources' (Kallis et al., 2015, p. 3), it also necessitates challenging capitalism as a political-economic regime based on accumulation (Foster, 2011; Saito, 2023) or any other form of 'growth society based upon the development of productive forces' (Latouche, [2007] 2009, p. 89). It goes without saying that social change of this magnitude would be difficult. Twenty-first century hubris, manifesting as humans' deep-rooted self-confidence regarding being able to engineer planet Earth (Hamilton, 2013) combined with capitalistic hegemony and the power of corporations (Suarez-Villa, 2009), ensures that a global transition to degrowth is close to impossible. Nevertheless, several small communities, operating with diverse drivers, have started to practice alternatives to growth societies (Joubert and Dregger, 2015; see also GEN, 2024). In line with what Kallis et al. (2015) listed as the primary significations of what a degrowth society might look like, these organizations are practicing voluntary simplicity, conviviality, self-sufficiency, and care by means of cooperation and sharing.

However, perhaps the most controversial question in both the practice and theory of degrowth concerns the question of *technology*. What kind of needs are there for technology in a degrowth society and on the route to achieving it? For example, is it necessary for us to communicate via the internet as much as we do or to travel by airplane? Some communication and travel are necessary, but how much technology is actually needed to maintain contact and to provide an occasional change of scenery? For instance, would it be enough to use video calls once a year and travel to distant destinations once a decade? Alternatively, what kind of technology is necessary to fulfil needs in a degrowth society? Might people connect by using the telephone and mail instead of higher-tech services such as Zoom and WhatsApp (be they commercial or open source)? Or might people talk face-to-face, or travel on foot to meetings? Would these satisfy the needs related to communication and travel in a degrowth society? Moreover, are they adequate practices to ignite the global degrowth transition? These questions, and many others related to technology, are highly important to us in the degrowth movement, and must certainly be answered sooner rather than later.

3. Ontic and ontological

For Heidegger, one of the most prominent philosophers of technology in the twentieth century, the above-mentioned questions only qualify as *ontic* questions as they are concerned with situational, tangible, and specific matters of technology (Heidegger, [1927] 2012). In order to clarify the phenomenon of technology, an enquiry must also enter the *ontological* register that underlies, and yet exceeds, the ontical. This signifies that before dealing with the more situational questions, we should be open to also examining the essence of technology:

We are questioning concerning technology in order to bring to light our relationship to its essence. The essence of modern technology shows itself in what we call enframing. But simply to point to this is still no way to answer the question concerning technology, if to answer means to respond, in the sense of correspond, to the essence of what is being about.

Where do we find ourselves brought to, if now we think one step further regarding what *enframing* itself actually is? It is nothing technological, nothing on the order of a machine. It is the way in which the real reveals itself as standing-reserve. (Heidegger, [1952–1962] 1977, p. 23)

4. Matter-energy throughput

As there are strong indications that economic growth is the main cause of ecological destruction, degrowth scholars call for economic downsizing in terms of decreased matter-energy throughput (e.g. Schneider et al., 2010; Martínez-Alier et al., 2010; Sekulova et al., 2013; Kallis et al., 2012; D'Alisa et al., 2015). Throughput, of which GDP/GNP/GWP at least used to be rough measures (Boulding, 1966), is 'whatever flows through a system, entering as input and exiting as output' (Daly, 1992, p. 333). For a degrowth analysis, the most important inputs are the so-called natural, non-human resources, while the central outputs are climate emissions and other forms of pollution.

It is important to recognize that '[t]he global average metabolic rate has doubled from 4.6 tons/capita in 1900 to 8–9 tons/capita at the beginning of the 21st century' (UNEP, 2011, p. 18). According to Schaffartzik et al. (2010, p. 87), the '[g]lobal average material use increased from 5.0 to 10.3 tons per capita and year (t/cap/a) between 1950 and 2010'. In this metabolic process of 'going through', *finite* matter-energy travels from states of low entropy to high entropy, and because of entropy, humankind cannot rely on resources always being in a form that facilitates their easy utilization (Georgescu-Roegen, 1975). According to the laws of thermodynamics, all forms of matter and energy become dissipated when used, and are hence less accessible to the users, humans.

In addition to the problems of resource (inputs) scarcity, the ongoing, fast-paced transformation of objects produces waste (output) at a rate that has undesirable ecological consequences. When forests are cut down faster than they renew themselves, it results in deforestation, the destruction of habitats, and the absence of carbon capture. When stocks of fossil fuels are burned in the atmosphere, it results in harmful emissions heating up the climate and it reduces air quality. The prevailing unsustainability is thus an effect of too intense a throughput. In other words, the matter-energy 'flow beginning with raw material inputs, followed by their conversion into commodities, and finally into waste outputs' is not 'within the regenerative and absorptive capacities of the ecosystem' (Daly, 1996, p. 28), underlining the urgency of the need for economic degrowth.

Schneider et al. (2010, p. 511) 'distinguish between depression, i.e. unplanned degrowth within a growth regime, and sustainable degrowth, a voluntary, smooth and equitable transition to a regime of lower production and consumption'. In physical terms (*physis*), a degrowth society is one whose throughput is made to decrease in order to avoid the depletion of natural, non-human resources (input) beyond their regenerative capacity and to avoid pollution (output) beyond the absorptive capacity of the bioregion. So, unlike growth economies, a high throughput is not desired in a degrowth society; instead, throughput is 'regarded as something to be minimized rather than maximized' (Boulding, 1966, p. 9). Moreover, since the reduction in throughput is incompatible with further economic growth, it will entail, in all likelihood, economic degrowth (Kallis, 2011). An ever-decreasing throughput, or degrowth, is not, of course, an end in itself but a means to a sustainable society (see Kerschner, 2010). In order to reach sustainability, degrowth societies are a necessary form of organization which economies whose throughput exceeds the sustainable scale must enter.

5. Techne and physis

The question of technology has perplexed sociologists and philosophers for several decades. One of the starting points for analysing the social side of technology was established by Heidegger. According to him, technology is not merely a means to achieve an end but also a human activity, 'a mode of revealing' (Heidegger, [1952–1962] 1977, p. 255). Despite the instrumental definition of *technology* being correct, Heidegger suggests there is a need for a broader (phenomenological) understanding of technology in order to comprehend its essence.

The etymological origins of the word *technology* can be traced to the Greek notion of *techne* (τέχνη). 'To the Greeks *techne* means neither art nor handicraft but rather: to make something appear, within what is present, as this or that, in this way or that way' (Heidegger, [1959] 2001, p. 157). '*Techne* is a kind of revealing or bringing forth—*poiesis*—belonging to craftsmen and poets' (Zimmerman, 1983, p. 108). So in the conceptual frame of Heidegger, ancient *techne* is the know-how that corresponds to the activity of *poiesis* (Di Pippo, 2000), the 'precondition for any kind of making' (Zimmerman, 1983, p. 108).

Another necessity for making something appear in the activity of *techne* is *physis*, or *phusis* (often translated as 'nature' in English), which forms the matter-energetic basis of being. Even though this remark is not explicitly stated in Heidegger's philosophy, he does consider that '*techne* and *phusis* belong essentially together' (Di Pippo, 2000, p. 32). Heidegger 'explains that the bringing forth of Being involved in human production is ultimately grounded in the bringing forth of *phusis*' (ibid, p. 32). Moreover, 'it is through the experience of the *poiesis* of *phusis* that human production takes its bearings and distinguishes itself' (ibid). In summary, *techne* can be considered to refer to the processes of revealing by means of making that are enabled by the physical, non-human world.

While the *techne* was characterized by Heidegger as a sort of poetic openness to the world, modern technology arose from the attempt to control the world and thus 'does not unfold into a bringing forth in the sense of *poiesis*' (Heidegger, [1952–1962] 1977, p. 14, also p. 131, xxv) but of something else. And the more humans began to seek control and believe in their power to master the laws of nature, the more modern the technology was developed.

In terms of the second precondition for *techne*, namely the physical basis of any activity of revealing, modern technology follows the ancient description: all technological activity requires *physis*. Unlike its earlier form, however, technology today places an unreasonable demand of supplying matter-energy for extraction and storage on the non-human world (see Heidegger, [1952–1962] 1977, p. 14). Partly due to this, the speed of bringing forth in the contemporary world has increased to an unprecedented level and making has reached a global scale (with drilling for oil in every corner of the world and experimenting with geoengineering being the most radical examples).

6. Standing-reserve

In the lifeworld dominated by technology, all matter-energy is taken as a resource, what Heidegger ([1952–1962] 1977, p. 17) aptly calls a 'standing-reserve' [*Bestand*]—and utilized for production. So fundamentally, 'the sway of [*techne*] does not consist [only] in manufacturing, but [also] in representing producing, such that what is handed over and what is deliverable secures calculating availability of the whole of everything with which what is produced right now is interconnected above all according to its producedness' (Heidegger, [1936–1944] 2006, pp. 154–155). It is through this constant producing that modern technology pursues its insatiable ambition 'to re-create the world' (Meagher, 1988, p. 163).

The essence of modern technology, according to Heidegger ([1952–1962] 1977), lies in enframing (*Ge-stell*). This 'Enframing means the gathering together of that setting-upon which sets upon man, i.e. challenges him forth, to reveal the real, in the mode of ordering, as standing-reserve' (ibid, p. 20). Heikkerö ([2012] 2014,

p. 5) explains this notion eloquently:

> In Martin Heidegger's thinking, 'enframing' (*Ge-stell*) names the framework within which Being is revealed during the technological epoch. Enframing refers to a way of disclosing the world. There is always such a way: in the Middle Ages, Being was unconcealed as creatures in relation to the Creator; in the modern age, Being becomes unconcealed as a resource (*Bestand*) to be used. Within enframing, modern science and technology disclose a truth about the world, but another way of disclosing would open the world differently.

Following Heidegger, I define technology through its ontological essence, *enframing*, a mode of human existence. I then conceptualize technology as practice. This conceptualization is an important precursor to examining the question of agency in technology and the related ethical implications.

7. Agency and social practices

The idea of a degrowth society is exceptionally revolutionary as it signifies a large-scale cultural change, including changes in social structures, values, and practices (Latouche, [2007] 2009). The transition is considered to be far from simple as it touches upon the very fundamentals of contemporary social organization, including the understanding of how this social change could take place.

The question of agency—the performance of doing and saying (Schatzki, 2002)—is assumed to be crucial in understanding change and the opportunities it offers. The notion of agency is often used to refer to an actor's ability and/or capacity to act in a specific situation by overcoming the structural and institutional constraints of the surroundings. While agency is conventionally theorized as a privilege of the rational human individual,[7] contemporary social studies stretch agency to include collective

---

7 Plumwood (2001) argued that the over-emphasis of human agency and under emphasis of non-human agency are traits of an anthropocentric culture: 'Hegemonic conceptions

entities (Lockie, 2004; Vincent, 2008; Schwinn, 2008) and non-human actors (Johnson, 1988; Barad, 2014), as well as human and non-human assemblages (Bennett, 2010). Moreover, the source of agency is often situated in social practices instead of simply attempting to explain change as a product of either the individual agent's traits or the structures surrounding the agent (see, e.g. Bourdieu, [1972] 1977; Giddens, 1984). 'All social action is a concrete synthesis, shaped and conditioned, on the one hand, by the temporal-relational contexts of action and, on the other, by the dynamic element of agency itself' (Emirbayer and Mische, 1998, p. 1004).

Taking a practice-theoretical view, social change is hence neither considered to be merely an outcome of the internal drivers of an agent, nor something caused by the external forces of social structures (Shove et al., 2012). Rather, change is fabricated in the practices of (more or less) amalgamated human and non-human agents that act within (more or less) amalgamated material and non-material structures. In other words, social practices are neither fully determined by structures nor fully free of them, making the old tug of war between proponents of free will and determinism unnecessary (Emirbayer and Mische, 1998). When agency is entrenched in practice, the opportunity for social change lies in the emergence, reproduction, and disappearance of practices making 'each present activity [...] potentially a new start, potentially itself a change or the beginning of change' (Schatzki, 2014, p. 17).

Moreover, as the social world is always in composition alongside materiality (Bennett, 2004), the 'future is made in the ceaseless advance of human and non-human agency' (Schatzki, 2002, p. 210). In other words, agency for change is highly relational and embedded in the nexuses of practices, as explained by Schatzki (2014, p. 17):

---

of human agency are fostered in human-centered culture; these are linked to denials of dependency, which in turn are linked to the application of inappropriate strategies and forms of rationality that aim to maximize the share of the "isolated" self and neglect the need to promote mutual flourishing' (p. 5).

This advance is not, however, a leap into an empty, unfurrowed, isotropic space that receives motion in any direction. Agency does not invent the future wholesale from its own resources. Instead, it arcs through a variegated and folded landscape of variously qualified paths: Agency makes the future within an extant mesh of practices and orders that prefigures what it does—and thereby what it makes— by qualifying paths before it. Indeed, the incessant advance of agency is the endless happening of the social site, from which nascent agency "starts" in the twin senses of originating (taking place) at and being formed as the doing it is.

This time and place in which agency is situated signify that different activities embed a varying degree of agency that is socioculturally mediated (Ahern, 2001) and that each agency 'varies considerably in different settings and societies' (Knappett and Malafouris, 2008, p. x). That is, agency is always contained within practices, and that being so, agencies take shape, and are shaped by, social practices. It is important to note here that change to a degrowth society must also reside in social practices rather than merely in the structures or values of agents. What counts is the change in practice.

8. Technological practice

In a pragmatically oriented analysis, technology can be, and often is, defined merely as an instrument (e.g. Georgescu-Roegen, 1975), which is justifiable; but Heidegger ([1952–1962] 1977) expounded a broader view of technology with enframing, one which includes the practices of 'manufacturing and utilization of equipment, tools, and machines, the manufactured and used things themselves, and the needs and ends that they serve' (p. 4–5). However, as Heidegger directed his main focus onto the phenomenal questions of being and existence, he paid less attention to the more practical sphere of technology. Nevertheless, Heidegger's early philosophy (alongside Ludwig Wittgenstein's later works) has been considered to offer a central philosophical background for the so-called theories of practice that analyse the social through everyday practices (Reckwitz, 2002; Schatzki, 2014). Although Heidegger can be read as a practice theorist, his view on modern technology was not very practice based. Thus, in order to study the implications of technology, Heidegger's work on technology should be connected to, and completed with, ontic investigations (something that can also be studied 'empirically').

Enframing manifests on the ontic register as practice, a technological practice. The term *technological practice* refers not only to the framework wherein the world unfolds as a standing -reserve but also to the kind of activity that emerges in parallel with (and as a consequence of) the mode of existence. This technological practice repeats and reinforces enframing, forming a sort of spiral of modernity. But while the technological practice 'responds to [...] Enframing, [...] it never comprises Enframing itself or brings it about', as Heidegger ([1952–1962] 1977, p. 21) pointed out. Furthermore, enframing as a human mode of being cannot contain or capture the technological practice in its totality as non-human objects are also involved in the lifeworld. Hence, there is always an element of surprise in the manifestation of Being.

9. Degrees of technology

In the task of understanding the role of technology in social change, the conceptualization of technology as practice seems pertinent as it is not limited to scrutinizing certain technological instruments from a benefit–harm calculus (which can also be considered a technological practice) but instead allows an enquiry to examine what technology (as a whole) is and does.

Theorists of practice have defined *technology* as a constitutive part of social practices. For Reckwitz (2002, p. 249), for instance, a practice is:

a routinized type of behaviour which consists of several elements, interconnected to one other: forms of bodily activities, forms of mental activities, 'things' and their use, a background knowledge in the form of understanding, know-how, states of emotion and motivational knowledge.

Technology, from this view, is merely an element of routinized behaviour. According to Schatzki (2014), the site of the social consists of practices, which are 'open spatial-temporal nexuses of doings and sayings that are linked by arrays of understanding, rules, and end-task-action combinations [...] that are acceptable for or enjoined of participants' (p. 15). In Schatzki's view, technology becomes conceptualized through material arrangements that are linked to social practices. Whereas Schatzki (2002) saw technology as arrangements that are co-produced with practices, but are nonetheless distinct from them, Shove et al. (2012) declared a more constitutive role for technology by positioning it as an element of social practice.

Drengson (1995) also used the notion of technological practice when developing his eco-philosophical approach to the study of technology. By studying practices, he identified different stages of technology, ranging from that of hunter-gatherers to agriculture, and onto industrial and information technology practice. In the descriptions of these stages, it becomes evident how technological practice is a product of its time and place, and how diverse degrees of technology can be identified.

So, to interpret technology as practice is to first acknowledge that technological practice varies in degree. While the definitions by practice scholars (e.g. Reckwitz, 2002; Shove et al., 2012; Schatzki, 2014) give technology a central role in organizing the social world, discussion about the degree of technology in practices seems to be implicit or non-existent. The notion of the degree of technological practice means that practices are either higher-technology practices or lower-technology practices. For example, swimming in the ocean can be considered a less technological practice than swimming in a heated, human-made, and maintained pool. Second, conceptualizing technology as practice, instead of assuming technology is just an element of practice, importantly broadens the analysis to include those activities that enable the specific technological practice being practiced. For instance, in the case of swimming, the manufacturing and heating of the pool are such enabling and provisory practices. As most theories of social practice would readily limit their analysis to technologies in use, questions on closely related and conditional object relations would attract less research attention (Rinkinen et al., 2015). This is not to say that theories of practice are silent on the questions of, for example, production and supply (see, e.g. Røpke, 2009; Mylan, 2015), but it does indicate that the analyses have emphasized technology as merely a part of daily practice. Conceptualizing technology as practice permits the exploration of a broader analysis scope. To recognize the cumulative and overlapping character of technological practices is central to assessing the criteria of measurement for how technological (as well as how matter-energy intensive) a certain practice is.

Lastly, the study of technology as practice does not lose sight of the essence of technology, the ontological realm of technology. To connect the technological practices back to the ontological register, it is arguable that the degree of technology depends on whether a specific practice more or less leads to enframing. This is of course impossible to assess in terms of grades as the essence of technology implies a specific mode of thinking and being. Thus, albeit the degree of technology can only be assessed on the ontic register of practice, ontological attention may reveal some of the fundamental, inherent limitations and expected directions of technology. According to Heidegger ([1952–1962] 1977), it is an illusion of modernity to think of technology merely in terms of a practice without seeing the essence of technology underlying the activity.

While an exponential increase in technology defines the history and present of our lifeworlds to an ever-greater extent, the continuation of such development is not predetermined. Contrary to what Heidegger ([1976] 1981) famously declared about the future on humanity, it is not only a god that can save us. Every situational action, including a departure from technological practice, is potentially a new start and a catalyst for social change, as Schatzki (2014) stated. However, in order to understand both who or what determines the degree and reach of technology in practice (and why they do so) and the possibility of social change and degrowth, we must turn to discussing the question of moral agency in technological practice.

10. Morality

'The pursuit of perfection and increasing power in technology practices, and the spread of technology throughout our culture, have now become so pervasive that it makes sense to call the twentieth century the Age of Technology' (Drengson, 1995, p. 86). While some may still consider technology something manageable and controllable, critical voices have declared the technological development to be autonomous and beyond human control (Ellul, [1954] 1973; Winner, 1977). For instance, 'Was the Fukushima nuclear facility, say unit 3, controllable before the tsunami and uncontrollable only after it?' Vadén (2014, p. 1) promptly asks, also supporting the view that technological practice can become self-directed.

According to sociologist and philosopher of technology, Jacques Ellul ([1954] 1973), technology has, in fact, come to obey its own laws, proclaimed itself as an independent agent, and rejected all other reasoning, including traditional morality:

> The power and autonomy of technique are so well secured that it, in its turn, has become the judge of what is moral, the creator of a new morality. Thus, it plays a role of creator of a new civilization as well. This morality—internal to technique—is assured of not having to suffer from technique. In any case, in respect to traditional morality, technique affirms itself as an independent power. Man alone is subject,

it would seem, to moral judgement. We no longer live in that primitive epoch in which things were good or bad in themselves. Technique in itself is neither, and can therefore do what it will. It is truly autonomous. (Ellul, [1954] 1973, p. 134)

In a similar way to Heidegger, Ellul ([1954] 1973) also goes beyond the instrumental definition of *technology* and sees modern technology as a totalizing phenomenon imposed on human activity that follows the single principle of the efficient ordering of things. Technological instruments and the practice of technology have certainly changed the way humans perceive and encounter things, be they objects labelled as belonging to the human, animal, vegetable, or mineral realms. Verbeek (2006), for instance, neatly illustrated how technological instruments are providing answers to ethical questions about how to act through the design of products and processes:

> Technologies are able to evoke certain kinds of behavior: a speed bump can invite drivers to drive slowly because of its ability to damage a car's shock absorbers, a car can demand from a driver that he or she wear the safety belt by refusing to start if the belt is not used, and a plastic coffee cup has the script 'throw me away after use,' whereas a porcelain cup 'asks' to be cleaned and used again. (Verbeek, 2006, p. 362)

This example also demonstrates how thin the line between the categories of technological instruments and practice really is. Technological instruments—as non-human agents—are able to direct change in practice by supporting a certain kind of behaviour over another. But despite the realization that technology can, and has, gained agency in today's societies, it is difficult to recognize how technology (whether examined as an instrument, a practice, or as any other phenomenon) could become fully autonomous, as suggested by Ellul ([1954] 1973) and Winner (1977).

From the technology-as-practice point of view, the agential

autonomy of technological instruments is difficult to adopt as it would denote that they are independent of all other elements of practice. As theorized earlier, while non-human agents may have agency, it is always entrenched in situational practices, and the human made always exists in relation to the non-human (see Latour, [1999] 2009; Schatzki, 2014). Moreover, the assumption that humans would be able to create a fully autonomous technological device is not empirically valid and seems to over-estimate human engineering capacity. As Drengson (1995, p. 48) put it:

> Saying that technology becomes autonomous implies that it takes on a life of its own. However, it has such a life only as a projection of our own shadows. Technology only appears to have its own inner life, dynamic, and logic. In reality it is driven by our own subconscious intelligence, and the crafty ego of its makers. These makers can be unaware that the 'autonomy' of technology is only a projection of the shadowy fragments of a larger self. This larger Self is hidden because the small self (ego) is not completely integrated with the whole context and is still engaged in defensive maneuvers.

In addition, to consider technological practice autonomous is quite troublesome as, according to Schatzki (2014), practices are always intertwined with other bundles of practices and hence have no clear boundaries. Thus, to say that a practice is independent of other practices loses its grounds. Each technological practice is not only dependent on all previous technological practices but also on other coexisting practices that are unfolding simultaneously. Every 'action is a concrete synthesis, shaped and conditioned, on the one hand, by the temporal-relational contexts of action and, on the other, by the dynamic element of agency itself' (Emirbayer and Mische, 1998, p. 1004).

However, technological instruments 'can both act by themselves in varied independence and structurally shape human agency' (Heikkerö, [2012] 2014, p. 28) as technological practice can direct thinking in the direction of enframing, as well as change behaviour. As Carlile et al. (2013, p. 8) noted, 'any form of agency is made all the more poignant by the fact that its consequences will be made material and can last over time', as in the case of a nuclear disaster, for example. An uncontrollable explosion in an atomic energy reactor shapes the affected human and non-human agency by setting limits to what doings and sayings can be performed, if any (in the case of fatalities).

Technology defined as an instrument has agency, while technology theorized as a practice embeds agency. However, the agency of and in technology is neither fully free nor determined; it only holds a degree of autonomy that is contingent on its context. Following Schatzki's (2002) train of thought, it could then be suggested that social change is made in the ceaseless advance of technological and non-technological agents. And when agency is entrenched in technological practice, the opening for change lies in the emergence, reproduction, and disappearance of the practices performed by the agents (Schatzki, 2014).

Even if technological instruments can assert a degree of agency, they do not meet the criteria of moral agents as 'to be a moral agent is to have the potentiality for living and acting in a state of tension or, if need be, conflict between two moral points of view' (MacIntyre, 1999, p. 318, see also 1981). Neither a machine, nor a hammer, has this potentiality. Furthermore, the lack of morality in the agency of technological instruments shows in their inability to make judgements and situational decisions instance by instance, which is considered a necessary condition for ethical conduct (Introna, 2009). The same deficiencies apply somewhat to *technological practice*. Rather than enabling its agents to deliberate on the issue of good and right (in a specific time and place), a technological practice directs the performance towards clarifying, arranging, and rationalizing, as well as integrating, objects by aiming to bring efficiency to everything (Ellul, [1954] 1973; Drengson, 1995). In technological practice, the world not only unfolds as a standing reserve in the minds of its human agents but the agency in technology is also geared towards an active, universal utilization of objects.

With this single aim of transforming by means of ordering (Ellul, [1954] 1973) and creating (Meagher, 1988) the world, technological practice does not support the emergence of moral human agency. However, what technological practice does enable is the calculative deliberation on different points of view (as long as they are within the essence of technology): enframing. In other words, technological practice allows people to ask questions with moral relevance, such as questions about what to do with the standing reserve, but it does not support its practitioners in working outside this frame where the world does not unfold as a means to an end.

While technological practice does not offer an exit from instrumentalization, it does corrupt its agents to varying degrees. It seems that the less technological the practice is, the less instrumentalization characterizes the agency; but by definition, technological practice does and cannot support the emergence of a kind of agency that either does or can let anything just be. Actually, it seems that the embedded agency in technological practice is insatiable in this respect. It constantly craves for more reordering of objects through its inherent determination to constantly calculate and make things from other things. Yet these actions often 'have a certain moral authority because they are taken to impose objectivity and neutrality in a complex domain that is already loaded with moral significance' (Introna, 2015, p. 23).

CHAPTER TWO
Releasement

This chapter claims that the needed antidote to enframing is releasement, the act of letting things be. By releasement, the world is allowed to unfold its complex genesis—the human intervention in worldly affairs and nature by means of technology is not always necessary. The ethos of releasement develops a new moral agency capable of withdrawing from technological practices. We are not confined to dwell enframing.

11. Meditation

With technological practice, human agents have come to exert a global-scale force on the ecosystem (Barnosky et al., 2011), leading to unforeseen rates of extinction of non-human species and, consequently, also leading to human agents jeopardizing the existence of humanity itself (Barnosky et al., 2012). In line with Introna (2009, p. 28), one 'could argue that it is morally unacceptable to create things that enroll us into programs that ultimately damage our environment or our fellow human beings', as technological practices currently do. Ongoing development calls for a radically alternative way of thinking about ethics (Introna, 2009) in order to guide social practices.

The present ethos of techno-capitalist cultures could be described as plutocentric due to the advocacy of economic growth over social and environmental concerns, but it could also be described as technocentric due to the strong belief in technological solutions (Ketola, 2010; see also Ulvila and Wilén, 2017). At best, proponents of the techno-capitalist culture engage in an overinclusive win–win–win rhetoric, in which the ecosphere ends up being the loser. What unites these three modes of ethics is anthropocentrism, the 'view that the non-human world has value only because, and insofar as, it directly or indirectly serves human interests' (McShane, 2007, p. 170). Both epistemic anthropocentrism, which considers humans as the only sources of value (or the only valuers), and moral anthropocentrism, which considers humans as the only locus of inherent moral value, are problematic. In a similar way to humanism, which 'proclaims the "right of man" and reduces everything else to the status of commodity' (Zimmerman, 1983, p. 100), anthropocentrism elevates the human species over other beings.

By doing so, the anthropocentric view grants ethical legitimacy to seeing the non-human world as a standing reserve for human ends, and as McShane (2007, p. 179) noted, it 'rule[s] out certain ways of caring as inappropriate to non-human objects.' Zimmerman (1983) even proposed that regarding objects merely in instrumental terms prevents humans from understanding the essence of objects. But most obviously, an anthropocentric approach to ethics fails 'because it assumes that we can, both in principle and in practice, draw a definitive boundary between the objects (them) and us' (Introna, 2009, p. 31). These points direct enquiry towards a non-anthropocentric ethos that allows the human and the non-human worlds to peacefully coexist and prosper on their own terms.[8]

Zimmerman (1983, 1994) and Introna (2009) have suggested that Heidegger's ([1959] 1966) notion of releasement (*Gelassenheit*) could serve as a basis for the needed morality. Peculiarly,

---

8 Zimmerman (1983, p. 102) suggested that 'Heidegger would agree that a non-anthropocentric conception of humanity and its relation to the natural order must go beyond the doctrine of rights [...]: Proper behaviour towards beings can only follow from right understanding of what beings are.' However, whether Zimmerman's interpretation is accurate is questionable as the categories of *anthropocentric* and *non-anthropocentric* are not employed in the works of Heidegger.

Heidegger himself was as much a critic of technology as he was of traditional morality. He was concerned that the very idea of morals could reproduce the thinking inherent in technological practice, where humans act towards an aim in a utilitarian sense. Releasement applied as an ethos is, however, still distant from any conventional ideas of morality. Borrowing the term releasement from Meister Eckhart, Heidegger's *releasement* offers exactly a break from the calculative thinking that has led humanity deep into technological practice:

> This letting-go means that we keep ourselves awake for releasement which, on the other side, means that we open ourselves to something, a 'mystery' that [...] is actually being itself, and is that which lets us in into *Gelassenheit*. (Dalle Pezze, 2006, p. 1)

For Heidegger, this mystery is 'hidden in the technological world' (Dahlstrom, 2013, p. 121) and hence 'humanity on Earth remains in danger of technology so beguiling that calculative thinking remains the only sort of thinking in use, the only sort of thinking that counts' (ibid, p. 122). Only with meditative (rather than calculative) thinking can human agents release themselves from technological practice and create spaces for new modes of relating, closer to being itself. Heidegger ([1959] 1966, p. 52–53) explained this meditativeness and its relationship with technology as follows:

> Is man, then, a defenseless and perplexed victim at the mercy of the irresistible superior power of technology? He would be if man today abandons any intention to pit meditative thinking decisively against merely calculative thinking. But once meditative thinking awakens, it must be at work unceasingly and on every last occasion [...]. For here we are considering what is threatened especially in the atomic age: the autochthony of the works of man.
>
> Thus we ask now: even if the old rootedness is being lost

in this age, may not a new ground and foundation be granted again to man, a foundation and ground out of which man's nature and all his works can flourish in a new way even in the atomic age?

What could the ground and foundation be for the new autochthony? Perhaps the answer we are looking for lies at hand; so near that we all too easily overlook it. For the way to what is near is always the longest and thus the hardest for us humans. This is the way of meditative thinking. Meditative thinking demands of us not to cling one-sidedly to a single idea, nor to run down a one-track course of ideas. Meditative thinking demands of us that we engage ourselves with what at first sight does not go together at all.

While Introna (2009) considered that an ethos of releasement is impossible, he remarked that it 'is exactly the impossibility that leads us to keep decisions open, to listen, to wait, and to reconsider again and again our choices—to let things be' (p. 42). This dependence on both calculative and meditative thinking is made evident when examining practices related to meeting basic needs. For instance, dwelling necessitates technological practice and instruments, as well as calculative thinking, to some extent. In human life, not all objects can be released from their use and be subject to mere meditative thinking. Some clarity, arrangement, and rationalization, as well as integration and efficiency, are needed in those everyday practices that are crucial to human existence.

The dilemma, however, is that technological practice does not support meditative thinking but rather encourages the calculative mindset to dominate. This is evident, for example, in the so-called micro-collapses when a technological practice is disrupted. As the technological practice alters from high-technology to low-technology—for instance, in the face of power cuts when centralized energy provision is replaced with localized low-tech solutions, such as wood stoves—new spaces unfold for reflection and change (Rinkinen, 2013). This may be due to having more time, a change in tempo, or an increase in autonomy and the altered possibilities for object control. What is important here is that the often unexpected collapses of technological systems imply that refraining from technological practice—either intentionally or by accident—is indeed necessary for a non-technologically dominated ethos and a non-technologically dominated practice to emerge.

12. Non-instrumentalization

Conceptualizing technology as practice has enabled us to look beyond technology as an instrument by broadening the scope of analysis to include the essence of the technological phenomenon (Heidegger, [1952–1962] 1977). The practice lens applied to technology (Drengson, 1995; Schatzki, 2002) also led to identifying degrees of technology, suggesting that practices can be characterized by having a lower level of technology or higher level of technology.

Varying approaches can be used in assessing the degree of technology, but for the present enquiry, the rate of throughput is decisive. When estimating the throughput necessary for any practice, the analysis ought to consider all the phases of technological practice, that is, the life cycle of a practice. It is of course impossible to arrive at a number for a specific technology as technological development is cumulative (Drengson, 1995) and the boundaries of a practice are in constant flux (Schatzki, 2002). A further complication results from the multitude of rebound effects in both time and place that forever escape measurement (Finnveden, 2000; Binswanger, 2001).

An intuitively plausible rule of thumb would suggest that the humbler the technological practice is in terms of the instruments used, the less ecospherical damage is causes. The practice of shelter building, for instance, is undoubtedly lower in terms of the level of its throughput when operated with convivial tools rather than machines (Illich, [1973] 2009) and fewer exosomatic instruments[9] (Georgescu-Roegen, 1975).

---

9 'Apart from a few insignificant exceptions, all species other than man use only

13. Hybridity and cyborgs

In terms of the instruments used in the practice of technology, it goes without saying that use of endosomatic (rather than exosomatic) instruments would have the desired consequences of decreasing the throughput of a practice. Walking instead of riding a bike or driving a motor vehicle is ecologically more sensible, as is talking (face to face) instead of speaking on the phone or via Zoom. This does not have to signify that humans have to stay where they were born but would certainly set some limitations to the ongoing mobility craze. On a larger scale, desisting from using 'advanced' exosomatic instruments would mean that humans would lose access to some matter-energy use (e.g. fossil fuels), which is desirable from the degrowth perspective. The longer artificial arms become, the deeper humans can drill into the Earth's crust, e.g. Furthermore, the more machines and systems evolve, the more humans tend to lose their agency in the vagaries of ever-more complex technological societies (Ellul, [1954] 1973; Winner, 1977).

If technological practice is given the ever-expanding role it craves, objects become more 'cyborgian' and the boundaries between made and born entities, anthromes and biomes, and the natural and the artificial continue to blur. That is, technological practice leads to dangerous homogeneity in both a cultural and an ecological sense as the ambition of the practice is exactly about transforming objects in order for them to obey the laws of the human calculated order. Most cultures are already deeply technological (Ellul, [1954] 1973; Winner, 1977), and the rationale for nature conservation is attacked. In the modern world,

---

endosomatic instruments—as Alfred Lotka proposed to call those instruments (legs, claws, wings, etc.), which belong to the individual organism by birth. Man alone came, in time, to use a club, which does not belong to him by birth, but which extended his endosomatic arm and increased its power. At that point in time, man's evolution transcended the biological limits to include also (and primarily) the evolution of exosomatic instruments, i.e. of instruments produced by man but not belonging to his body. That is why man can now fly in the sky or swim under water even though his body has no wings, no fins, and no gills.' (Georgescu-Roegen, 1975, p. 369).

characterized by technological practice, there is little 'nature' left (as noted by several post- and ecomodernization theorists) and, hence, also no objects to be considered 'natural' (or 'wild' or 'organic') that would need to be sustained or released from technological practice.

It surely is true that things are assuming more and more hybridity, as human-made objects are 'crowding out the environment' (Daly, 2005, p. 100). When thinking about this, it is important to remember that it is precisely technological practice that is behind this change. Every engagement in technological practice intensifies the accumulated throughput, the overall amount of objects transformed through human instruments and hands.[10] That is, as technology is practiced, objects are forced to travel past the social sphere and transform into a new state in order to benefit the human species, but not necessarily the whole ecosphere. (This practice is legitimized by anthropocentrism.) In entropic terms, this means that technological practice always results in a deficit as 'the cost of any biological or economic enterprise is always greater than the product' (Georgescu-Roegen, [1970] 2011, p. 52). Further, the greater the degree of a technological practice, the greater the deficit. A less intensive technological practice, again, allows a larger number of objects exist outside the use.

14. Refraining

An alternative practice that goes beyond modern technology is surely necessary for the twenty-first century. 'We need a new way of understanding Being, a new ethos, that lets beings manifest themselves not merely as objects for human ends, but as intrinsically important' (Zimmerman, 1983, p. 99), and releasement offers this. Heidegger posits that 'we should respect all beings not because they resemble humans, not because they are

---

10 Endosomatic evolution may also increase entropy, but the amount and speed are arguably far lower than with exosomatic evolution.

valued by humans, not because they are experienced by humans, but because they are what they are' (ibid, p. 122). Zimmerman (1994, p. 132) explains the practical implications of releasement as follows:

> First, it means not unduly interfering with things. Second, it means taking care of things, in the sense of making it possible for them to fulfill their potential. Third, letting be involves not just the ontical work of tending to things, but also the ontological work of keeping open the clearing through which they can appear.

According to Heidegger ([1959] 1966, p. 55), releasement 'grant[s] us the possibility of dwelling in the world in a totally different way'. In the current situation, where technological practices continue to have severe ecospheric consequences (see, e.g. Drengson, 1995; Parkes, 2003), it seems that the transition to degrowth necessitates the ethos of releasement to a large extent. An ethos for degrowth must be strongly connected to a frame of thought that allows non-human objects to unfold not as a standing-reserve but on their own and hence manifest their complex genesis.

One way to releasement could be to cease to partake in those practices wherein the essence of technology dominates. Participation in technological practice, including its calculative mode of thinking, reinforces the embedded agency for more technological change. This signifies a shift from active engagement in multifarious technological practices that necessitate a global production and distribution network to conviviality (Illich, [1973] 2009), which is rooted in a region. 'The region gathers—just as if nothing were happening—each to each and everything to everything else, gathering all into an abiding while resting in itself' (Heidegger, [1944] 2010, p. 74). Openness to releasement through meditative thinking may denote not only a change in the degree of technological practice and instruments (quantity) and the kind of technology (quality),[11] but may also unfold as *atechnology*.

Releasement offers a plateau upon which new ethics can emerge, but the interpretations and conceivable political consequences of it warrant careful consideration and must be implemented with caution. As Zimmerman (1983, p. 102) puts it:

> Humanists would argue that it is politically dangerous to abandon the principle of human rights in favor of the obscure notion that we should 'let things be,' while some radical environmentalists would maintain that Heidegger himself remains a humanist because he overestimates the importance of the human being's supposedly unique ability to speak.

At first, it is possible to think that this alternative ethos that calls for letting things be may lead to passivity in the face of injustice— be it the recurrence of fascism in Europe, the global march of neoliberal capitalism, or the extensive destruction of species' habitats. However, as Heidegger ([1944] 2010, p. 70) himself noted in *Country Path Conversations*, the releasement of things lies 'outside the [very] distinction between 'activity and passivity'. Maybe it is possible to talk about deliberate inaction or active passivity in the case of an ethos for encountering the non-human world. This is because, in order to reduce matter-energy throughput, it is exactly the collective refraining from technological practice that is the indispensable act. To have a degrowth society, a great volume of fossil fuels must be left in the ground, a vast portion of forests must

---

11 A solar panel, for instance, is certainly a different instrument in terms of its quality than a coal plant, but the quantity is a key issue for matter-energy throughput. Because of the bio-physical base of our existence, even solar panels cannot be produced without limits. A single coal plant on the planet is not a problem, but a billion factories manufacturing solar panels certainly would be. Based on this rationale, it could be suggested that for degrowth, it is ultimately a question of quantity. For Heidegger, however, a central question was quality: the unlocking of energy. 'The revealing that rules in modern technology [...] puts to nature the unreasonable demand that it supply energy that can be extracted and stored as such' (Heidegger, [1952-1962] 1977, p. 14). An old windmill, for example, does not do this as 'its sails do indeed turn in the wind; they are left entirely to the wind's blowing' (ibid). It appears that Heidegger did not see the matter-energetic limits of building windmills.

be left to grow, and most fish must be left in the oceans. For the ecosphere to recover, human activity must shrink. An answer to the important question of 'Does the degrowth movement need technology?' begins to take shape. Is there a need for more clarification and arrangement, calculation, and assessment, as well as more organization, rationalization, mechanization, computation, digitalization, artificialization, and integration of objects with the predefined aim of having control and bringing efficiency and order to everything? The short answer to the above question is no. 'Under this regime [of technology] the mechanistically defined world becomes primarily a storehouse of raw material and a source of power for the engines of industry to turn out commodities and services for the market' (Drengson, 1995, p. 88). It is hence somewhat evident that a degrowth society needs neither technology as a general frame that manifests in the increasingly technological practice nor new instruments. The world is already full of the tools and artefacts required for dwelling. In fact, the converse can be considered the case. In order to reach degrowth in terms of decreased matter-energy throughput, practices must shift away from technology. Releasement is the only way out of technology (Heidegger, [1952–1962] 1977).

Given the prevailing unsustainability, I argue that expectations of technology being a means of delivering ecologically sensible change should be reconsidered in a critical light. Consequently, the book calls for humans to refrain from employing the technological frame and technological practice. While this is difficult because most of us are deeply entrenched in the routines and habits of technological society, there is always an opportunity for change. Schatzki (2007, p. 17) explained this constant flow of opportunities:

> each present activity is potentially a new start, potentially itself a change or the beginning of change. Whether present activity is a new start depends on what is done and how others react to this.

Moreover, it follows that, similarly to ethics, meditative thinking cannot be above or detached from practices, but must rather unfold within the plenum of practices (see, e.g. Schatzki, 2002; Introna, 2009).

15. Against eco-fascism

Somewhat paradoxically, the reasoning I offer would probably be a re-enactment of technological thinking for Heidegger as it describes things in terms of their purpose or aim. This book claims that in order to attain degrowth in terms of decreased matter-energy throughput, practices must shift away from technology. And yet, here I am participating in those practices.

To problematize the setting even further—from the very framework of the chapter—is to remark that this book (as an object) is also human-made, which means that the process of making the claim has caused an increase in the cumulative throughput. In fact, quite a lot of matter-energy was first perceived as a standing reserve and then used in order to complete the study. In the practice of letting be, fewer academics and arguments are undoubtedly needed and created as meditativeness is even beyond language, the chief human-made object. Releasement leads to stillness and meditative presence. That being so, this book should not be taken as an example of practicing releasement or even as a Heideggerian interpretation of technology. Building on the works of, inter alia, Heidegger, I present a viewpoint on the relationship between technology and degrowth.

As the book is built on the minimalist definition of *degrowth*, namely the reduction of matter-energetic throughput, it is important to acknowledge additional limitations of the approach. 'Being concerned with resource scarcity, or with ecosystem destruction, but not with world justice can lead to top-down anti-population proposals and anti-immigration discourse' (Demaria et al., 2013, p. 206). The present book by no means seeks to put forward an eco-fascist message; in fact, it does the opposite.

Refraining from technological practice is perceived as a way of ensuring that any form of totalitarian organization is ungovernable. As the present and history so vividly demonstrate, the transition to (as well as the maintenance of) a fascist regime would almost certainly need technology. In fact, totalitarianism and fascism can be seen as manifestations of the very essence of technology. But how can a radical confinement to a region, which is an almost inevitable consequence of moving to a lower degree of technological practice and the use of less exosomatic instruments, not end up being a form of exclusive localism defined by intra-species conflicts? This is a central question for the future enquiries into technology and degrowth, wherein it would be worthwhile to maintain the locus of attention on exploring the practice of releasement, in particular in relation to social skills.

16. Atechnology

It is interesting, and possibly ironic, that humans have survived precisely because they have adapted their environment by means of technological practice instead of simply becoming adapted to it, but now it is observable that the transformation of the non-human world that humans have brought about is jeopardizing human survival, as well as other species.

This book has described what technology is and how apt technology is for prompting degrowth. Technology is defined as enframing, a mode of being, which manifests in technological practice of different degrees. Rather than strictly saying 'yes' or 'no' to technology, the question concerning technological practice for degrowth seems to largely be a question of degree. Are there not too many non-human objects being transformed into human-made ones via technological practice, conducted with too many technological instruments? As ecosystems collapse around us, there is a wealth of empirical evidence to support the view that the human species has gone too far in terms of transforming nature. To reach degrowth in terms of decreased matter-energy throughput, practices must be geared away from the technological frame of thought to a considerable extent.

At its simplest form, this book argues, technological practice does not support degrowth as it directs its agents towards the continuous transformation of non-human-made objects into human-made objects. Nature is turned into anthromes, anthropogenic mass. In a manner challenging to the quest for the desired change, which requires degrowth, the transformation of objects (undertaken in technological practice) signifies an increase in cumulative throughput. The more technological the practice, the fewer things are released for use. Even the transformation of existing human-made objects into new objects (recycling) needs matter-energy and contributes to the overall metabolic load on the Earth. Hence, contrary to ideas about ecological modernization, the book claims that an increase in the degree of technological practice signifies an increase in matter-energetic throughput. Therefore, the chapter strongly challenges the dominant position of technology as a means for sustainable change and calls for refraining from technological practice by means of the new ethos: releasement.

CHAPTER THREE
Transformation

This chapter claims that transformation discourses, as well as the following other practices, are problematic as they lack an analysis of human will. To enact sustainable change, the seemingly insatiable human (w)ill to transform, including the paradox of trying to conserve nature by transforming it, must be understood and treated.

17. Sine qua non

Albeit the movement encompasses a variety of political and philosophical ideas (Kallis et al., 2012; Demaria et al., 2013; Sekulova et al., 2013), the minimum requirement for the degrowth condition is a reduction of matter-energy throughput. But whether the transformation discourse will take this *sine qua non* seriously is another question. There is at least a danger that the debate on transformations will not support the revolutionary aims of degrowth and instead become another buzzword in the conceptual toolkit of reformers and quasi-radicals. Consequently, the 'transformation' will be about seeking to decouple economic growth from ecospheric harm through further technologization. As a questionable, yet likely, outcome of such a conceptual hijack, the understanding of what actually needs to change and how, would not be altered significantly (see Bonnedahl and Heikkurinen, 2019).

Signs of this kind of lack of rigor can be identified in the transformation literature as 'analytical clarity is often superseded by visionary and strategic orientations' (Brand, 2016, p. 505). If instead of offering vague conceptual connections between sustainable means and ends, a more explicit and solid theoretical perspective is presented and applied to transformations, there seems to be a tendency to employ a rather one-dimensional view of change. Somewhat typically of the transformation literature, Wright (2013, p. 2), for example, assumes that it is 'institutions and social structures and processes' that are central to transformations.

Such a structuralist perspective emphasizes the role of governance arrangements and appears to have a strong foothold in thinking about transformations. Even in the context of the emerging degrowth theory, 'the majority of [...] proposals are national top-down approaches, focusing on government as a major driver of change, rather than local bottom-up approaches' (Cosme et al., 2017, p. 321). This is not only problematic in terms of providing a theoretically weak explanation of how change takes place, it is also a challenging position in terms of practice as the current age of neoliberal techno-capitalism is known for the amalgamation of the public and private spheres of human action (see, e.g. Scott, 1998; Lazzarato, 2005). That is to say, the so-called democratic structures are largely steered by markets and driven by the interests of capital.

But how should the necessary transformative changes then be conceived and conceptualized in order to contribute to degrowth? Aiming to advance understanding and debate on this question, this chapter begins by analysing the idea of transformation and problematizing its underlying drive: the human will to transform. The chapter then moves on to outline a phenomenological response for triggering profound changes in the spirit of degrowth beyond this will.

18. Transformative change

Among the chapter's key claims are that the discourse on transformations is mainly ontic (as it emphasizes 'the social' or 'the political' as the source of change). 'Ontic is an adjective that Heidegger uses to designate a specific entity (or specific entities) as well as the description, interpretation, or investigation of it (or them). Heidegger contrasts an ontic investigation with an ontological investigation that is directed at disclosing an entity's manner of being as such' (Dahlstrom, 2013, p. 146). That is, ontic questions are concerned with situational, tangible, and specific matters, while ontology deals directly with being (Heidegger, [1927] 2012). In line with Heidegger, this chapter assumes that to gain a more complete understanding of the phenomenon of transformation, an enquiry must also enter the ontological register that underlies the ontical world.

By doing so, it leaves aside ontological questions (relating to being) that are crucial for the understanding of change of great magnitude. The ontic investigations encourage thinking about what should be transformed in the socio-political sphere, as well as how that should be undertaken and when, but do not permit questioning of the transformation itself. Examining transformation beyond the ontical makes it clear that while the transformation discourse has its technical and theoretical issues, the main problem is the insatiable urge to endlessly 'transform' the world that underlies the call for transformations. Building on Nietzsche's ([1882] 2001; [1883–1888] 1968) notion of the 'will-to-power', I conceptualize this drive as the 'will-to-transform', so shedding light on the source of the transformation discourse.[12] I propose that the observation that humans experience an urgency to transform the world, while this transformation is at the same time a root cause of the ecospherical crisis, should be called 'the transformation paradox'.

The manner in which Karl Polanyi uses the concept of transformation in *The Great Transformation* does not convey anything positive or desired but rather the contrary. For him, the notion of a great transformation primarily refers to the rise

---

12 Li's (2007) critique of the will, in the form of the will to improve social conditions through development interventions by a broad array of (more of less) colonial actors, resembles the idea of the will to transform that is outlined in this chapter. An in-depth analysis is needed in order to map the synergies between studies problematizing the will in relation to issues of social justice, on the one hand, and environmental justice, on the other.

of market liberalism that led to the Great Depression and the rise of fascism in Europe. For him the great transformation was thus a significant event in human history that marked the move to a more efficient economic growth paradigm from the earlier society. Polanyi saw the transformation to this system of self-regulating markets as so complete that he considered it to resemble more 'the metamorphosis of the caterpillar than any alteration than can be expressed in terms of continuous growth and development' (Polanyi, [1944] 2001, p. 44). His definition of a transformation is also reflected in the more recent theorizing on transformations where a 'transformation is [...] understood to mean a *profound, substantial and irreversible change*' (Brown et al., 2013, p. 100, emphasis added). However, the contemporary call for transformations that resonates broadly with actors from both the public and private spheres, and also with the organizations of civil society, is significantly different to Polanyi's concept of transformation, namely that the new great transformation is nothing historical but a future being made. But even if a generic description of a transformation as a revolutionary change rather than a reformist change could be agreed upon and taken as an important aim for the modern condition that is characterized by planetary-scale destruction of the ecosphere, what change will actually be considered 'profound, substantial, and irreversible' will largely remain moot. To outline some parameters for distinguishing *transformative change* from other kinds of change, the chapter will investigate the term in more detail.

19. Reform

The etymology of the word *transformation* dates back to the mid-fourteenth century. The Latin origin word *transformare* signified a change in shape, a conversion of an object. Its prefix 'trans' refers to 'across', while the latter part of the word, *formare*, is about forming something. If compared to its conventional conceptual pair of *reform*, which refers to forming something again, *transformation* signifies a very different type of change (in both quality and quantity). These two basic working definitions indicate that that transforming is about changing the form itself, while reforming would be about rearranging the form. Moreover, to transform is to bring forth a new form that includes novel elements not limited to the human sphere. In other words, a genuine transformation not only refers to human doings but, as noted by Blok (2011, p. 114), 'requires that we drop our everyday way of life' and 'dwell by the happening of clearing and concealment.' Again, to reform is to reuse the already available elements and reordering them to make a somewhat different kind of form. In this sense, transformation resembles the processes of art (*techne*), which 'concerns the bringing forth of *gestalt*' (ibid, p. 101). 'Bringing forth, however, is not exclusive to art: the making of equipment is also a bringing forth and this explains why the Greeks use the same word, τέχνη [*techne*], for handicraft and for art' (ibid, 2011, p. 105). Consequently, present day transformations must be viewed as having their roots in the ancient concept of *techne*, even if the power of *logos* has changed the process tremendously. That is, transformations today are largely technological.

It is important at this point to further distinguish between the human-induced modifications of the form (both reformations and transformations) that are to a great extent technological, and then metamorphic change, which is not a product of human will or mastery. The difference can be clarified by thinking about the metamorphosis of the caterpillar to the butterfly. The same entity in the matter-energetic reality assumes an entirely different shape, and almost nothing in the entity remains the same. Crucially, it is not only the caterpillar (as an agent of change) that desires a new formation, there are other forces (beyond the agent and its will) that enable this shapeshifting to take place. Metamorphosis is not an anthropogenic 'transformation'. It is also noteworthy to remark that human activity, particularly the techno-capitalist activity, has affected not only the ontic but also the ontological shifting (that is, there is an ontology of techno-capitalism which makes claims about being) (Jones, 2016). This makes the problem both human and cultural—the intention to *reform* and *transformation* is mainly (but not only) an ontic *intention*, while *metamorphosis* has a stronger ontological connotation.[13] In phenomenological terms, the metamorphosis is a *gestalt* switch. This bears similarity with the experience of fictional salesman Gregor Samsa. In his book *Metamorphosis*, Franz Kafka's protagonist wakes up in the morning and finds himself mysteriously metamorphosed into an insect.

Thinking about change as being ontical places the focus on that which is factual, in physical terms, and is therefore certainly important for considering how to reduce matter-energetic throughput. On the spectrum of current proposals for change, the degrowth movement (with its focus on matter-energy flow) is certainly more transformative than reformist. However, the problem with limiting the analysis to the ontic issues (or similar) is that doing so does not grant access to being itself, and consequently, any understanding, even about the ontic, remains very partial.

But similarly to Heidegger's idea of human being (*Dasein*), degrowth—as a human enterprise—'is ontically distinctive in that it is [also] ontological' (Heidegger, [1927] 2012, p. 32). Owing to its inclusive spirit, this means that degrowth is both ontical and ontological, or *ontico-ontological* (a term that Heidegger uses in describing human being [ibid]). Accordingly, for the sake of clarity, it is meaningful to contrast 'ontic degrowth', referring to particular issues in relation to the actual reductions in matter-energy throughput, with the unfolding 'degrowth ontology'. But before this chapter immerses itself into the ontological, it will shed light on the concept of transformation from the ontic perspective.

---

13 While reforms and transformation are considered ontic, the metamorphosis discussed in this chapter concerns being. Nevertheless, a metaphysical understanding of form, which Heidegger too would reject, is not intended here (see Blok, 2011).

20. Transformation paradox

It is particularly the paradoxical nature of the call for transformations, wherein human-induced change is simultaneously the cause of ecospherical problems yet considered to be the solution to them, which demands closer scrutiny. The transformation of nature,[14] measured in matter-energetic throughput, is identified as the foundational problem of unsustainability (see, e.g. Kerschner, 2010; Bonaiuti, 2011; Kallis, 2011). That is, at its simplest, the ecospherical imbalance can be distilled to the overuse of so-called natural resources or capital and the resulting emission of too much waste in various forms, such as greenhouse gases, that the global and local ecosystems cannot absorb. In this way, at the core of unsustainability is the fact that too much nature is transformed and brought deeper into the human sphere, which ecological economists refer to as *human-made capital* (see, e.g. Daly, 1996). For example, rivers are being turned into power generators, fossils into gasoline, and stones into skyscrapers.

Georgescu-Roegen (1975) held that the rate of transformation can be measured in terms of the matter-energy that travels through any organization or culture. Usually, the degrowth solution to the problem of a too extensive rate of transformation is the transformation of the social (see, e.g. Latouche, [2007] 2009; D'Alisa et al., 2015; Asara et al., 2015). By way of explanation, to have a successful transformation to a degrowth society, the amount and rate of transformation from nature to the human-controlled sphere must radically decrease, and slowing down this metabolic flow of matter and energy requires a change to the socio-political

---

14 The position of the present chapter in defining *nature* is that all earthbound phenomena are embedded in nature (see, e.g. Heikkurinen et al., 2016). Hence, 'nature is that [all] which we observe in perception through the senses' (Whitehead, [1919] 1964, p. 2) or the whole (von Wright, 1978; 1987). While the blurring of the boundaries between, e.g. humans and non-humans must be acknowledged, they are still considered to be important analytical categories for the degrowth movement. The gradual disappearance of the constructed boundaries between these categories (i.e. hybridization or cyborgization) does not make the categories void and useless.

order. It is after all, certain kinds of social values, practices, and structures that are considered to define the so-called metabolic flow of human societies.

While this is true, there is a paradox. The embeddedness of human enterprises in nature makes all social, political, and cultural activity dependent on the matter-energetic basis of the ecosphere, leading to a painful enigma in the call for transformations for degrowth. The so-called transformation paradox emerges from the thermodynamic fact that all human-induced transformations require further non-humans to be transformed. Scilicet, matter-energy which humans cannot create is always needed for action. Every human action, such as changing the fossil-based technological infrastructure to fit renewable energy or even organizing a demonstration, requires matter-energy and hence increases entropy. And the more transformative action there will be, the more matter-energy will be required. But even if these acts of an individual or a collective (e.g. scholars flying to conferences) do not compare with the planetary-scale problems (e.g. CO_2 emissions), the two are related in a very direct manner as the macro is the cumulative outcome of the micro. This all means that paradoxically, in the process of making social transformations happen, which are considered to be the solution to ending growth, there is a need to continue transforming nature, which is the source of further growth.

One of the arguments to counter the paradox is to think that there are 'good transformations' and 'bad transformations', and that the bad ones can and should be replaced with the good ones. This is very similar to the 'green growth' narrative (see Lorek and Spangenberg, 2014) and 'sustainable growth' narrative (see Daly, 1990) as well as to the 'good Anthropocene' narrative (see Hamilton, 2016), which encourages humankind to keep transforming things but doing so differently and producing items of better quality. The basic problem with the transformative agenda is that it does not challenge whether the acts themselves should be undertaken at all but seeks to improve those acts with enhanced techniques and enlightened goals.[15] For example, academics would not have to quit or even replace their scholarly work with low matter-energy action (such as meditation or dancing), they could just do better scholarly work at the institute while the matter-energy intensity remains unaltered (or may even increase). From a degrowth perspective, such an improvement could be a neoclassical economist transitioning into ecological economics or a scholar publishing a more critical article whilst their other activities remain the same.

Accordingly, to avoid confusion about what should not be transformed, it is vital to acknowledge the difference in the transformation of human-made nature (e.g. social values, practices, and structures) and the transformation of non-human nature (e.g. mountains, lakes, winds, bacteria, and birds).[16] This distinction is important because what is being transformed and what is not makes a great difference in the context of degrowth. As Daly (1996) remarks, since humans are not able to substitute for non-human processes and capital, a critical stock of them must be maintained to enable human existence (see also Holland, 1997). However, as the non-human and the human spheres are not separate from the earthbound whole in neither ontic nor ontological senses, these two can only be separated for analytical purposes, such as doing so in order to make sense of the transformation discourse.

---

15 In terms of ethical theory, this thinking has close resemblance to utilitarianism in which the speculated net benefit of the expected consequences can be used to legitimize harmful means.

16 The notion of non-human nature here refers to entities and processes of nature which are not human induced or anthropogenic. The boundaries between these two spheres are increasingly vague as human activities now influence almost all earthbound beings and processes of nature (see, e.g. Abram, 1996). Consequently, it is more precise to consider the human–nature relation as a processual continuum rather than a static dichotomy or dualism wherein the current movement is towards having less non-human (or more-than-human) nature on Earth.

21. Critique of action

To this point it has been argued that an anthropogenic transformation always necessitates further transformation of the non-human as human action is not autonomous from the rest of nature. All human systems on Earth derive their vitality from the non-human sphere by transforming matter into energy and energy into work. Because of the human dependence on nature, the call for transformation is a call to take an entity (e.g. a forest, oil, or lithium) and use it for some human purpose, such as to discharge humans from physical labour. However, even if human action cannot be reduced to the flow of matter-energy, it is nevertheless contingent on non-human entities and processes. Even to *think* about being independent of matter-energy, one needs food and water, as well as shelter. But because thinking (as a mode of action) surely requires substantially less transformation of non-humans than almost any other human action, perhaps meditative refrainment should be emphasized at times over the impulse to just act more in order to meet the minimum ontical requirement of the degrowth movement, that is, reduced matter-energy flow.

The old environmentalist slogan about thinking globally and then acting locally could be recast as: *think local; reflect; think global.* The urge to quickly act upon the ecospherical crisis is certainly understandable given the realization of the scale of the anthropogenic catastrophe that the Earth is enduring; however, the caveat involved is that by undertaking more actions, one may further escalate the problems, particularly as human activities are so intertwined with economic processes of growth.[17] From

---

17 The rebound effect, or Jevons paradox, illustrates this intertwinement (see Alcott, 2005). The key observation here is that the improvement of the quality of human activities (e.g. efficiency by means of technology) does not necessarily signify lower matter-energy throughput. Examples of how such a rebound can occur can be given in the context of household energy systems. Changing old incandescent light bulbs to new LED bulbs can mean less energy is consumed when using the lights, but the overall energy consumption of the household may remain the same (or even increase) due to this alternation. This is because the 'saved' energy is used elsewhere. The rebound effect is augmented in a market economy, where a decrease in demand tends to lower prices in order to bring back the temporarily reduced demand.

the viewpoint of the Earth, it is precisely *less human action* (not only better action) that is needed. In a similar fashion, even if from a very different perspective, Žižek (2012, p. 1) criticized the contemporary fetishism of action, suggesting that there is a need to 'start thinking' and 'not get caught into this pseudo-activism and pressure to do something [...], the time is to think'. Nevertheless, of course, some action is essential in order to provide the metabolic requirements of the human species' everyday survival, that is, in order to meet the basic needs of water, food, shelter, sleep, and sex. It goes without saying that subsistence-related practices will always have priority in the world over abstract thinking and reproducing the scholarly discourse, however transformative and radical the latter claims to be (cf. Max-Neef, 1991).

In the spirit of degrowth, it is therefore of primary importance to ask what the direct matter-energetic consequences of human actions targeting degrowth are. How destructive to nature, for instance, is the kind of thinking that manifests in producing the transformation discourse. With its million-dollar research projects and conference travel, the work of creating the transformation has not only become a profession for many academics, consultants, managers, politicians, and civil servants, but has also created an industry with a growth imperative of its own. This cultural criticism may feel rather beside the point but is in fact at the core of the (ontic) argument so far. Another key observation is that the call for transformations may end up being very reformist unless the matter-energy reduction requirement is taken seriously, including as it relates to the activities of the degrowth proponents. In this respect, the degrowth movement is not an exception to any other agent of change: the ends still do not justify the means. And since all human action increases the metabolic flow of societies, reflection on which actions to undertake (which are relatively low in terms of throughput) is vital in the already overshooting growth society.

However, it is not the intention of this chapter to encourage a cost–benefit calculus and turn the human–non-human relationship into a vast harm–benefit exercise.[18] Instead, this chapter intends to show that the common response to the call for transformation by accelerating action, be it political influencing, academic work, ecopreneurship, or non-governmental activity, always has some negative matter-energetic consequences. In entropic terms, this means the acts of humans always result in a deficit as 'the cost of any biological or economic enterprise is always greater than the product' (Georgescu-Roegen, [1970] 2011, p. 52). Phrased as simply as possible: the more human action, the more chaos in nature.

The main problem of the transformation discourse then appears to be not its technical and theoretical problems, identified in the previous literature (see, e.g. Brown et al., 2013; Brand, 2016), but the transformation itself or, to be more accurate, the human actions that lead to further transformation of nature. That is to say, for the purposes of degrowth, both the amount *and* kind of transformation are the problem as all human-induced transformations require more transformation of nature. The simple solution to this is to undertake fewer transformations, but that is easier said than done. Before examining potential solutions, it is important to understand what drives transformations.

22. Will-to-transform

By transforming nature, humans have taken their place on Earth as a global force. In fact, this insatiable drive to conquer and master the planet (Hamilton, 2013) can be considered to characterize humankind, the luxurious animal, as Nietzsche put it. It is important to note, however, that humans have not contributed equally to the transformation of non-human nature, with the contribution of the high-consuming classes being

---

18 First, the so-called positive impacts of human activities on the non-human sphere are impossible to evaluate, if they even exist in the first place (see Ehrenfeld, 1978; Pauly, 2014). This is mainly due to the apparent limits of human knowledge about nature as a whole, in particular in the Anthropocene, as boundaries between humans and non-humans are increasingly hazy. Secondly, being human in the world is much more than optimization; human life cannot be reduced to any single principle or goal.

prominent (Ulvila and Wilén, 2017). Some humans and societies are obviously more luxurious than others. But in addition to identifying capitalism (Foster, 2011; Martínez-Alier, 2009), productivism (Latouche, [2007] 2009; Baykan, 2007), and technology (Heikkurinen, 2018; Samerski, 2018) as the three main causes of the present ruin, this chapter investigates the ontology of transformations across 'the triad'. It proposes the will-to-transform as a focal characterization of what drives transformations and growth, and consequently, what has led the planet to the state of ecospheric overshoot. Moreover, the roots of capitalism, productivism, and technology can all be drawn out from this inherent drive of humans to transform the social. As some of these may also encourage the will, they are not mere causes but also consequences—adding cyclicality and processuality to the phenomenon.

In line with the Nietzschean hypothesis of the 'will-to-power' (*der Wille zur Macht*), this chapter assumes that humans—among other beings—share a primary desire for power (Nietzsche, [1882] 2001; [1883–1888] 1968). While this interpretation of the will can be contested on grounds that include no one, not even Nietzsche, ever explicating its specific meaning (Porter, 2006), some general characteristics can be outlined. 'From the beginning of the second half of the 1880s, Nietzsche proclaimed explicitly that all reality is will to power', suggesting that there is only one intrinsic quality in reality (Aydin, 2007, p. 25). 'According to Nietzsche, the will to power is the fundamental feature of life and ultimately of the universe itself, i.e. it is Nietzsche's answer to the metaphysical question of what Being as such is' (Blok, 2017, p. 24).

For Nietzsche, power is relational: 'power in relation to another power' (Blok, 2017, p. 26). Without this power, causing something would not be possible. It seems that this relationality is not only a quality of humans, there is a will to power that constitutes the identity of all matter-energetic entities. In the human–nature relationship, this power to cause changes in the world is not problematic per se. That is, the fact that humans have the knowledge and skills needed to create great causes in the world, as evidenced during the Anthropocene, does not have to signify that power is used. In practice, however, this of course has not been the case, but at least it is something imaginable. Humans would not have to use their power but to refrain from using it. For example, even if someone possesses the will to have the power to cause harm, and gradually acquires that power, it does not automatically follow that person will use the power to harm or to do anything at all. It is not until the will to power is established and turned to use— to a drive and enactment to transform things—that it becomes problematic for degrowth.

Blok (2017) distinguishes between the will to power 'as truth' and the will to power 'as art'. Both of these drives have their roots on an ontological register, constituting the identities of earthbound beings. 'The will to truth is a necessary condition for life, i.e. for the continuation and preservation of life amidst contingency and change' (Blok, 2017, p. 25). And hence, it is the stabilizing side of being. Moreover, the will to truth can be considered 'a necessary but not a sufficient condition for life, because it is insufficient for the enhancement and growth of power. Nietzsche therefore says that we are in need of art in order not to be destroyed by the truth' (Blok, 2017, p. 25). It is then the will to art that enables the transgression of the stabilized identities towards a new form, *gestalt*, or mode of being (Blok, 2017), like the 'superman' (*Übermench*) in the work of Nietzsche ([1883–1891] 1997). This distinction is important for the present enquiry as it highlights the internal tension in the will to power that can also be found in the will-to-transform. It also shows that the will to art (*techne*) closely resembles the will to transform that underlies modern technology, even if they also have disparities (see Heikkurinen and Hohenthal, 2024).

23. Nietzsche

The will, both in the form of the will-to-power and the subsequent will-to-transform (the use of the power) can be considered to lie beyond good and evil: they just *are*. However, the enactment of these wills does have matter-energetic consequences that can be considered ethically more or less desirable. Moreover, similarly to the will-to-power, the will-to-transform is a hypothesis, but one arguably built on an extensive base of empirical evidence. In the rapidly expanding transformation discourse, the will to transform the social life of humans (and hence also to influence the rest of nature) is an unequivocally stated value axiom and considered a main objective of responsible human activity. 'We need to change everything!', the popular motto echoes. This interpretation of the human condition is slightly different from Nietzsche's ([1882] 2001; [1883–1888] 1968) as, according to him, humans do not have the drive to transform, but they hold on to the will-to-power as truth. Accordingly, the change that Nietzsche has in mind is to move from this will as truth to the will-to-power as art or as transformation. Painfully, the problem that Nietzsche did not foresee with his route to transgressing the animal rationale was the limits that matter-energetic realities set for the human will to transform. There are thermodynamic consequences of making art, as well as limits to making art.

Emerging from the Nietzschean will-to-power, the will-to-transform can be described as that force that pushes humans to endlessly craft and reorder the world. In terms of thermodynamics, this rearranging always requires matter-energy, and as an outcome of the activity, the Earth gradually moves from a state of lower entropy to one of higher entropy or, in other words, the Earth moves from order to chaos. The will is deep discontent to the present order of things and affairs, a desire to leave a mark, which arguably derives its meaning from the assumption of progress. According to the largely accepted premise of progress, the purpose for the human being comes from efforts to move humanity to an improved or more developed state or to a forward position. In Nietzsche's work ([1883–1891] 1997), this was the ambition of overcoming the contemporary human condition (*Übermensch*); therefore, constant transformation is needed, and stillness is not an option as the future is assumed to be a better time and place.

24. Techno-capitalism

It is quite reasonable to think that it is also because of this will-to-transform that technology has become the prevailing mode of being, something Heidegger ([1952–1962] 1977) referred to as enframing (*Ge-stell*), and it is why the ideology of private ownership and the accumulation of wealth has become hegemonic, to use the Marxian expression. That is, without the will-to-transform, humans would not have developed such advanced means of changing the world and its nature. Due to their transformative desire, humans have now made great achievements, such as modern science and techniques, that offer in exchange ever better knowledge, instruments, and the frames for transformative action. By means of technology, humans have been able to transform more, both in terms of quality and quantity. In addition, neoliberal techno-capitalism has been an extremely apt frame for organizing the efficient transformation of nature into a social, anthropogenic form. In the pre-modern age, the human focus was more on the will-to-power as truth, albeit certainly including some elements of the will to art, but in the contemporary age, the focus has shifted to the will-to-transform, leaving the question of truth aside. In the total mobilization (see Blok, 2017, p. 10–11) of techno-capitalism, the term *truth* is something used with the prefix *post*.

The main emphasis of the present epoch has been on the accumulation of wealth by means of advancing techno-science. All human activity—including scientific enterprise, which used to be about understanding truth—must legitimize its existence in relation to applicability and relevance to technological progress and economic growth. Affluence, in fact, has been accumulated at a rate that arguably no other system would have been capable of sustaining. However, like capitalism and technology, the will-to-transform is something that both has different degrees and is contingent on cultural and biological patterns. That is, some human cultures have (had) a more insatiable determination to constantly alter and rearrange things than others.[19] Techno-capitalism (see Suarez-Villa, 2000; 2009) is perhaps the most obvious example of the strong will-to-transform, where no being escapes this human drive and where values, practices, and structures are made to support the will to make a change happen. The economic discourse, which builds on the assumptions of consumer power to make transformative changes and the notion of the entrepreneur as a superman, vividly illustrates the will.

---

19 The assumption is that while there are differences in human cultures, all human cultures
have the will to transform to some extent. Owing to its conceptual nature, the chapter
cannot provide an empirical account of the factors that determine the extent of the will
to transform. What can be noted—based on the work of geographers, anthropologists,
and sociologists—is that different explanations apply to different contexts. The position
of the present chapter on this question is that the degree of the will to transform,
as well as change in general, is dependent on (at least) a bundle of different agential
characteristics, and social practices and structures, defined by both cultural (human) and
environmental (not limited to human) factors.

CHAPTER FOUR
Metamorphosis

*This chapter claims that by releasing the will-to-transform,
the reduction of matter-energy throughput becomes concrete and
possible. Non-willingness signifies waiting without an object, as well
as preparing for the expected, the collapse of matter-energetically
intensive cultures.*

25. Hope

With Nietzsche's will-to-power it is difficult, if not impossible, to
trace the will, or lack of it, to a historical point in time or place.
Therefore, the roots of the destructive growth machine can be
considered to run as deep as those of humankind itself. But even
if the will can be seen as a central aspect characterizing the human
species, the intention is not to reduce the human condition to
this will-to-transform but to question the origins of the real-
life existential problem related to the ongoing mass extinction of
life. It can nevertheless be said in the light of history that some
individuals have not developed the pathological versions of the will
and that some cultures have not supported the progress of the will
as much as others have.

Perhaps this is where 'hope' can be found in these dark times;
there are circumstances under which humans are able to let go
of, as well as to resist, their will to transform. But to envisage an
alternative mode of being, the analysis must be steered towards
a more personal stage (even if it is one that is not necessarily

individualistic), where the responsibility of actors is called into question. Owing to the ontological will to power and to transform that underlie the techno-capitalist system, the matter-energetic metabolism of societies will not change unless there are changes in the ways being itself is understood, which is consequently accompanied by a shift in beings' thinking and activities. As already indicated by Nietzsche, the liberal economy is embedded in the ontology of the will-to-power, to which I propose to add the will-to-transform. Therefore, to have radical change, one must also pay attention to the substitute ontological register of experience, ontology.

26. Non-willing

In his later work, Heidegger realized the need to move away from (or beyond) the will. For Heidegger, 'the will itself is the main barrier for the experience of "being"' (Blok, 2017a, p. 82). According to Arendt ([1971] 1978), Heidegger considered this, as he witnessed the destructiveness of the will, which 'manifests itself in the Will's obsession with the future, which forces men [i.e. humans] into *oblivion*' (p. 178). The will can thus be considered to be deep discontent with the present, which helps us to explain the emergence of this insatiable drive to transform and constantly alter the order of things in the world. Heidegger furthermore assumed 'the will to rule and to dominate is a kind of original sin, of which he found himself guilty when he tried to come to terms with his brief past [*sic*] in the Nazi movement' (Arendt, [1971] 1978, p. 173). So, in his later work, he makes an effort to repudiate this will in its entirety and becomes willing not to will. Heidegger describes this as follows: 'Non-willing means […] willingly to renounce willing. And the term non-willing means, further, what remains absolutely outside any kind of will' (Heidegger, [1959] 1966, p. 60).

The translated terms that Heidegger used to describe a way to repudiate the will were 'letting-be', 'letting-go', or 'releasement' (*Gelassenheit*). 'The mood pervading the letting-be of thought is the opposite of the mood of purposiveness in willing' (Arendt, [1971] 1978, p. 178). Having borrowed the term from a mystic, Meister Eckhart, Heidegger's *releasement* offers a break from the will, which is characterized by calculative thinking. As an activity, this letting be 'is thinking that obeys the call of Being' (Arendt, [1971] 1978, p. 178). 'This letting-go means that we keep ourselves awake for releasement which, on the other side, means that we open ourselves to something, a "mystery" that [...] is actually be-ing itself, and is that which lets us in into *Gelassenheit*' (Dalle Pezze, 2006, p. 1). That is, 'we may release, or at least prepare to release, ourselves to the sought-for essence of a thinking that is not a willing' (Heidegger, [1959] 1966, pp. 59–60). Hence, releasement 'is both the end and the required means for twisting free of the will; this is the aporia of the transition to non-willing' (Davis, 2007, p. 207). It is about moving away from the representational towards 'eco-poetic relations, intermediated via a presencing, atmospheric sensitivity and dwelling in proto-contemplative tunings and mindful practices' (Küpers, 2016, p. 1443).

Following Heidegger's concept of releasement, people and cultures that have left being as the will-to-transform can be referred to as *releasers*. In other words, releasers are practitioners of letting-be as they allow beings to unfold their complex genesis rather than considering them a standing-reserve to be transformed for anthropocentric, human purposes (such as economic growth). In relation to the will-to-transform, releasers are those individuals and collectives who are already moving from having more will to transform to having less will to transform. Their being has undergone a metamorphosis.

In ontic terms, this kind of turning in being manifests importantly in decreased matter-energy throughput or in less consumption, distribution, and production as beings are not transformed but left untouched (Heikkurinen, 2018). That is, owing to the lack of enacted will-to-transform, a decreasing amount of matter-energy is involved in human activities. Importantly for the degrowth movement, what follows is less extraction from nature, less production and use of goods and services, and also less disposal and waste. On the aggregate scale, the consequence is that the metamorphosis of being causes the metabolic flow of human societies to slow as less matter-energy travels through human hands and tools. And it is exactly because of this desired matter-energetic outcome of releasement that those who are releasing cannot be considered to equally contribute to the Anthropocene problem. It is their transforming co-humans (*transformers*) that cause the metabolic acceleration and, thus, further destruction of the non-human world.[20]

27. Releasers versus transformers

This distinction between releasers and transformers is important in assigning blame and distributing responsibility, as well as in imagining a proper response to resisting the destruction of growth, which at its simplest, means bringing transformations to a halt by means of non-willing. From the point of view of reducing matter-energy throughput, whether a person or a collective stops transforming by choice or by force does not make a great deal of difference because the direct outcomes are similar whether people reduce throughput because they do not have access to the required resources or because they choose to do so for deliberate and sophisticated reasons. However, with an extended time horizon, the will comes into play; for instance, if the required resources are made available to a person who has not possessed them before and who has the will to transform, it is then likely that he or she will make use of those acquired means. Therefore, the ontological metamorphosis, which includes releasement, is indispensable for the degrowth movement that is seeking to make societies stop short of transgressing the ecological limits.

---

20 While affluent areas and regions (in terms of GDP) have more transformers than the deprived ones, transformers are not limited to any particular spatial location, race, class, or religion. In addition to spending, wealth could be considered to indicate persons' and households' will-to-transform. This of course is limited to techno-capitalist cultures, in which monetary rewards are measured in relation to those actions that most effectively contribute to profit, competitiveness, and economic growth.

To illustrate this point further: there might be a person who does not currently possess the mental, monetary, and other reserves needed to make transformations happen, but as they gets 'well' (in the frame of progress), the will-to-transform can be expected to return. However, if that person has intentionally released, or willingly renounces willing, in the words of Heidegger, the change is arguably more permanent in ontic terms. Thus, despite the desired ecological outcome of his or her 'sickness', which is reduced matter-energy use, which in the case of suicide would be close to zero, they would not necessarily qualify as a releaser. As mentioned above, Heidegger refers to releasement as wanting un-willing.

To quote Heidegger ([1959] 1966) on this subject: 'You want a non-willing in the sense of a renouncing of willing, so that through this we may release, or at least prepare to release ourselves, to the sought-for essence of a thinking that is not a willing' (p. 60). But such a metamorphosis requires a call of being to which human beings can have the possibility. '[O]n our own we do not awaken releasement in ourselves' (Heidegger, [1959] 1966, p. 61). That is, the shift from being a transformer to becoming a releaser is not something than can be forced and is beyond mere human agency. And as Heidegger expressed, we should be calm about it (*gelassen*) precisely because we cannot enforce a call and have to wait for such a call of being. It is not anthropogenic.

The question arises as to what extent individuals and collectives, such as the degrowth movement, can really get rid of the will and undergo a metamorphosis in being. Perhaps Heidegger was too aggressive when he sought to completely eliminate the will and also too absolutist with his statements about human agency or the lack of it. After all, as Blok (2018, p. 33) noted: 'This self or identity of the one who wills is not autonomous or free in the strict sense of the word, as is confirmed by scientific research, but interconnected and interdependent with that which is willed in willing'. The task, therefore, must be a collective one, if anything. In addition, any kind of determinism is not a sound position in relation to the practice of releasement. For example, Heidegger's ([1976] 1981, p.

57) famous statement, 'Only a god can save us', does not reflect a meaningful take on human agency, but a rather one-dimensional view that could not accommodate the degrowth movement.

While pessimism about the future and the present condition of humans is acceptable, the practice of releasement cannot be based on an extreme of assuming free will or determinism. In other words, there must a degree of agency or autonomy that can be directed to independent thought and action, even if only in relative terms (Heikkurinen et al., 2016; Heikkurinen, 2017a). The nature of being 'does not imply that the act of willing is fully determined by that which is willed' (Blok, 2018, p. 33). What this signifies for the practice of releasement is that it is neither fully possible, nor fully out of reach. How much it can actually be reached, 'the degree [of agency], depends on the external (e.g. physical objects or cultural norms) as well as on the internal (e.g. mental models or self-imposed duties) restrictions' (Heikkurinen, 2017a, p. 459).

28. Waiting

Up to this point this chapter has argued that the ontological human will-to-transform manifests ontically in the transformation of nature to human objects, anthromes. Consequently, the will is a focal problem underlying growth, which has led the Earth to the Anthropocene. Each act of transformation requires natural resources, and the utilized matter-energy input problematically increases waste in the ecosphere (or *entropy*, in the parlance of thermodynamics). This being so, a proper response to the call for transformations would involve following the example of releasers, who allow being to unfold without constant anthropogenic intervention. That is to say, rather than running after the ontical transformations in the social, a metamorphosis in being is invited to complement the understanding of when and where not to intervene in the entities and processes of nature.

If the current analysis is correct, then releasers (who have already absorbed a degree of releasement) can be the harbingers of hope for the degrowth movement and perhaps even more that just hope as they are already living the metamorphosis through practicing releasement. But an important question remains: how can transformers become open to the experience of releasement? Davis (2007, p. 221) is worth quoting here at length:

> The 'house of being' modern [hu]man inhabits is constructed within the domain of the metaphysics of will. Yet it is not possible to simple vacate the premises overnight and take up lodging elsewhere. To enter into genuine dialogue with non-Western languages or to learn to speak in new ways requires going *through* the hallways and clearing the portals of our current domicile. Hence, if we are to open a window onto another vista, indeed if we are to build a pathway for transporting and rebuilding our house in a region beyond the domain of the metaphysics of the will, we must begin by learning to use the furnishings available in this house otherwise.

It follows that while the metamorphosis from transformers to releasers is of crucial importance, it cannot be rushed. The roots of the will-to-transform run deep and the contemporary mode of being is very pervasive. According to Heidegger ([1959] 1966, p. 62), 'we are to do nothing but wait' [*warten*] . He noted that we can get close to being released through waiting, '[...] but never awaiting, for awaiting already links itself with re-presenting and what is re-presented' (ibid, p. 68). Dalle Pezze (2006, p. 97) remarked that '"waiting" is the key experience, for when waiting we are in the position of crossing from thinking as representing to thinking as meditative thinking. By waiting, we move from that thinking which, as Heidegger states, has lost its "element" (be-ing) and dried up, to the thinking that is "appropriated" by its "element" (be-ing itself) and which, therefore, has turned towards be-ing itself'. Therefore, turning to releasing may unfold through waiting without expecting, so to speak or, as Heidegger puts it, '[i]n waiting we leave open what we are waiting for' (Heidegger, [1959] 1966, p. 68). This kind of waiting is already releasement (Davis, 2007).

29. Preparing

But perhaps Heidegger is again too strict about proposing to merely wait. After all, closeness to being cannot be reduced to a single task or practice, an observation that applies to the degrowth movement as well. Therefore, in addition to waiting, humans can do other things with a low matter-energy throughput, such as dance and meeting their primary needs, but in parallel, they might begin preparing for the expected that has already shown itself to many. Owing to the rigid path dependencies in the current techno-capitalist system, peak oil, and the political disinterest in curbing economic growth and over-consumption, a foreseen future is the collapse of human civilization (see, e.g. Tainter, 1990; Duncan, 1993; Tomlinson et al., 2013). As Evans (2005, p. 1) phrased it: 'We would be foolish to take for granted the permanence of our fragile global civilisation'.

Alongside the preparations for collapse, there are some practical implications that are linked to releasement. Zimmerman (1994, p. 132) explained these as 'not unduly interfering with things', but 'taking care of things, in the sense of making it possible for them to fulfill their potential.' For him, 'letting-be involves not just the ontical work of tending to things, but also the ontological work of keeping open the clearing through which they can appear' (ibid, p. 132). The people living in increasingly popular ecovillages and in transition towns seek to interfere in the non-human processes mainly to fulfil their primary needs for food and shelter (LeVasseur and Warren, 2019). This phenomenon of voluntary simplicity and self-provisioning is of course not limited to rural or semi-urban environments but is also apparent in urban settings. These practitioners' 'essential reasoning here is that legal, political and economic structures will never reflect a post-growth ethics of macro-economic sufficiency until a post-consumerist ethics of micro-economic sufficiency is embraced and mainstreamed at the cultural level' (Alexander, 2013, p. 287).

30. Paxcene

The great turning around that Heidegger referred to has already begun, but it might only gain momentum as the collapse proceeds. In his book *Heidegger and the Environment*, Rentmeester (2016, p. 61) noted that 'Heidegger often calls this great turning around a "new beginning" or the "other beginning" in that it will incite a change in the human relationship with being'. 'This new beginning is a radical departure from the previous epochs, though it somehow has a relation to the first beginning' (ibid, p. 62). The turning around, however, is not merely human-induced and also involves forces beyond the merely human (cf. Bannon, 2014). Perhaps the on-going collapse will take the Earth to the next geological epoch, which will hopefully be characterized by peaceful coexistence between humans and the rest of nature. This imaginary epoch could be optimistically labelled the 'Paxcene' (with the *pax* coming from Latin, denoting 'peace'), even if this will be far from *Pax Romana*.

Without modern technology and the growth of the global capital flow, the Paxcene is likely to region, funnel people where food and shelter are available. The purpose here is not to argue for a romantic, pre-industrial nature that humans could go back to but rather to direct some thought to the post-industrial era that will follow the peak of the collapse, which may—as beautifully phrased by Dalle Pezze—that which regions [*Gegnet*] '[...] creates, or perhaps reveals, a space/time, an expanse in which things themselves also do not have the character of objects anymore. They lose their nature of means and return to their nature of being as tree, stone, flower. They return to that moment that seems to be the absence of time—in the sense of sequence of moments—and emerges as time-space within which they simply are and rest'.

A way to understand this metamorphosis is in terms of the emergence of a new understanding or mode of being, that is, who we humans are (see Brown and Toadvine, 2012; Bannon, 2014). It is perhaps something similar to that which happens when leaving Plato's cave or when the caterpillar turns into a butterfly: it is a *metamorphosis in being*. It is not only a kind of Marxist emancipatory project for the worker or even the classic environmentalist task of saving the world, it is also consciousness unfolding in conjunction with those who wait and reflect. In a Heideggerian sense ([1952–1962] 1977), reflection is not just making oneself conscious of something and different from scientific or intellectual knowing. It is more. 'It is calm, self-possessed surrender to that which is worthy questioning' (ibid, p. 180). Moreover, '[r]eflection is needed as a responding that forgets itself in the clarity of ceaseless questioning away at the inexhaustibleness of That which is worthy of questioning—of That from out of which, in the moment properly its own, responding loses the character of questioning and becomes simply saying.' (Heidegger, [1952–1962] 1977, p. 182). This kind of Heideggerian ([1936–1944] 2006) mindfulness (*besinnung*) could be a path leading out of the Anthropocene.[21]

From the ontic point of view of reducing matter-energy in a complex world, things are relatively simple: those who transform the most are the biggest offenders and the chief part of the problem. In the light of natural sciences, and the laws of thermodynamics in particular, this assertion (even if it is reductionist) is difficult to reject; but *being* certainly does not reduce to the ontic need to reduce matter-energy throughput. In other words, the world is not merely about any binary or continuum, such as releasers versus transformers or the good versus evil, even if it is about binaries too. In fact, claiming such dualism would neither do justice to the present argument, nor (and more importantly) to the issues at stake in the late Anthropocene.

---

21 Even if this book calls for reflection on being, explanations of the current ecospherical crisis through economic relations and imbalances of power, as well as conventional calls for political change without an ontological rift, are neither a waste of personal time nor unimportant for the degrowth movement. For example, geographies of degrowth in an ontic sense, such as outlining strategies for radical reconfigurations of state–society relationships are considered complementary perspectives to the mainly ontological analysis performed in this chapter.

31. Context

Furthermore, for the geographies of degrowth, sensitivity to place is of crucial importance. Consequently, in the theoretical nexus of these two fields of study (namely degrowth and geography), a 'place' does not reduce to a phenomenon that is disclosed in personal, regional, national, and global spaces, it also encompasses earthbound geographies wherein the planet and the human condition are investigated in relation to degrowth (see Georgescu-Roegen, 1975). That is, in addition to a variety of multi-scalar contexts on the planet, 'the Earth' is also a place of relevance, belonging, and culture. This place, where nature unfolds as a whole, is located in the space of the cosmos (see Boulding, 1966).

The main contribution of the present analysis to geographies of degrowth is hence the following. By providing a conceptual analysis of the human will, the chapter proposes that while place sensitivity is vital to effectively reducing matter-energy throughput (as most of the production is for the wants of the global northerners), the problem of the disturbed metabolic flow on Earth cannot be reduced to any single cultural and empirical context. Thus, onto-spatial analyses of actors (as well as their relations and actions) that are bound up in the geography of the planet—in contrast to merely examining sub-planetary societies (e.g. nation states or particular regions)—complements the geographies of degrowth.

The will-to-transform, however, is also shaped by contextual factors such as race, class, ethnicity, gender (see Collard et al., 2018), and its manifestations are contingent on access to different forms of resources (e.g. economic, social, and cultural capital) (see Bourdieu, 1986), as well as influenced by the availability of natural capital (see Daly, 1996). The enactment of the will-to-transform can be supported and corrupted by power relations and exposure to ideologies of growth, such as capitalism (see Scott, 1998). As an empirical analysis of which of the cultural factors determine the degree of the will-to-transform was outside the scope of this chapter, this is an important next step for further studies. What is already known from previous studies is that the high-consuming cultures and individuals are the biggest burden on the environment due to their high matter-energy demand. The will-to-transform, however, is not limited to any particular income class (like the top 5% or 0.05%) even if the richest ones are doing most of the ecospherical damage (see Ulvila and Wilén, 2017).

Therefore, perhaps the most central issue for future inquiry (from a degrowth point of view) is to empirically examine how certain communities and individuals have denounced the will, and how this could be introduced to the over-consuming societies. Furthermore, by conceptualizing the will-to-transform, the present chapter calls for research to move beyond the dichotomy of 'the good' (often us) and 'the evil' (often them) in order to investigate the different degrees of the *will* to transform. In addition to examining others' (e.g. capitalists') will-to-transform, the chapter invites everyone to reflect on their will-to-power and transformation (as well as the other consequences of these wills) in the context at hand. Empirical analysis of the will-to-transform could hence also include auto-ethnographic studies and auto-phenomenographies as fruitful ways forward in the quest of understanding *being degrowth* and *degrowth being* it their diversity that is, the quest to understand degrowth as modes of being.

CHAPTER FIVE
Nature's cultures

This chapter claims that the place of all human cultures is in nature. No human can 'go to nature' as they are already there. All cultures belong to nature. This is an embedded view to the naturecultures debate. It is a misperception to think that because humans have become separated from nature, we experience alienation. This chapter validates that we can be estranged from nature while in nature, if nature has a core.

32. Exosomatism

The ecospheric crisis is considered to be a result of human failure to relate to nature (White, 1967; Næss, 1987; Foster, 2000). Previous studies, however, have also questioned the relevance of using the term *nature* due to its universalizing character and suggested that the perceived alienation or estrangement is *cultural* (Bookchin, 1962; Vogel, 1999; Biro, 2005). These competing explanations are also reflected in the current debate on the philosophical basis of the degrowth movement. On the one hand, the movement is influenced by deep ecology, which posits that humans are matter-energetically embedded in nature. On the other hand, the movement gains insights from social ecology, which tends to denaturalize the debate on the ecospheric crisis.

In the light of the state-of-the-art climate science (e.g. IPCC, 2013; 2023; Cook et al., 2016), the crisis is largely anthropogenic. That is, humans are to blame for the disturbances in the local and global ecosystems (e.g. temperature rise and its byproducts: melting ice, rising sea levels, extreme weather conditions). It is important to note, however, that fault and responsibility cannot be distributed equally as capabilities and power are unequally distributed across humanity (UN, 1992; Vitali et al., 2011). In other words, certain cultures (their individuals and organizations) have contributed more than others to climate change and biological annihilation (Chancel and Piketty, 2015; Oxfam, 2015; Ulvila and Wilén, 2017). Nevertheless, in comparison to other earthbound species, humans appear very exceptional as a group. Regardless of how fair the species unit of analysis is in terms of social justice, the havoc this single species has created does not compare to anything else in nature.

According to Georgescu-Roegen (1975), a central tenet that explains how humans become diverted from the rest of nature is their extensive use of so-called exosomatic instruments, like clubs, which do not belong to their bodies by birth. He referred to the tools that humans are born with, legs and hands for example, as *endosomatic instruments*. This cultural turn from endosomatic to exosomatic instrument use was a decisive point in the evolution of the human species, and is something that is considered to separate humans from other species and earthbound entities. It also divides cultures within the human species.[22] From this we could think that it is 'exosomatism' that defines humanity.

While there are also non-human animals that make use of exosomatic instruments, the degree is much lower and fewer when compared with human cultures. The contemporary, highly technological human organization is of course an extreme manifestation of high degree of exosomatic instruments (Ellul, [1954] 1973; Drengson, 1995; Heikkurinen, 2018). It has arguably become so dependent on complex technological systematizations that many of its individuals would not survive an abrupt collapse

---

22 For instance, the number and quality of exosomatic instruments varies greatly in indigenous and colonial cultures.

in the energy and food supply. Domesticated cultures gradually lose the skills needed for meeting basic human needs, which makes them more vulnerable to the absence of inputs from the global economy. This trend, however, is not limited to humans, but it is inevitably connected to humans. That is, pets and other domesticated animals would have difficulties to survive and prosper in a collapse scenario, whereas cockroaches, frogs, and wolves certainly would not mind an internet shutdown (or some other drastic event that would paralyse most humans), even if they all spatially (in metric proximity) live rather close to humans. There certainly is great variance between human cultures (e.g. between a colonial and indigenous culture), but there is a mysterious link to only human cultures. Non-human animals cannot cause the same effects as humans, perhaps exactly because of their use of mainly endosomatic instruments.

It is noteworthy that without the exosomatic turn, the emergence of complex humane cultures, such as emergence of the current neoliberal techno-capitalism that is penetrating the globe and beyond, would not have been possible. While some might consider high modernity an achievement of humankind, the human expansion in nature has come with severe costs. The techno-capitalist system destroys species' habitats at a faster rate than any other human enterprise in the past (Hoekstra et al., 2005; Zalasiewicz et al., 2008; Barnosky et al., 2012). These changes in nature cannot be overlooked by merely relying on the development of ever-more advanced exosomatic instruments that are capable of correcting the damage (Georgescu-Roegen, 1975; Drengson, 1995; Heikkurinen, 2018, see also Samerski, 2018). Instead, the relevance of seeking to overcome nature by means of technology should be critically assessed. Whether or not the exosomatic turn was *the* decisive point in the evolution on Earth, it has at least significantly altered the way humans relate to (the rest of) nature.

Hitherto, I have defined *degrowth* as matter-energy reduction and *humans* as a species characterized by extensive exosomatic instrument use or technology. The third key concept, namely nature, is again considered to stand for all earthbound phenomena. Following the traditions of ecology, as well as those of environmentally sensitive economics, sociology, and philosophy— *nature* is defined as the earthbound whole in which humans are embedded (see, e.g. Boulding, 1966; Murphy, 1995; O'Neill et al., 2008). Nature is earthbound, connected first and foremost to planet Earth.[23] In terms of having an epistemological stance on nature, the chapter draws on Whitehead's ([1919] 2005, p. 2) formulation. 'Nature is that [all] which we observe in perception through the senses', but it is not limited to human perception. As human cultures are embedded in nature, all that they perceive is nature. This, however, does not mean that humans perceive nature completely or that nature is only what humans perceive. Yet, nature unfolds in perception.

Before conceptualizing *nature* any further, the chapter analyses the feasibility of a rather conventional premise regarding human–nature relations, namely human alienation or estrangement from nature, as well as addressing some ethical issues related to the concept of nature.

33. Alienation

In ecological thought, the contemporary human condition is often characterized as 'alienation' or 'estrangement' from nature (Tolman, 1981; Dickens, 1997; Hailwood, 2015). The idea itself, and its present-day interpretation, is indebted to Hegel, Feuerbach, and Marx, but as a phenomenon, alienation surely goes beyond. Anyhow, if humans are considered to be embedded in nature, as proposed here, this process is a product of nature itself, as noted already at the turn of the eighteenth and nineteenth century by Hölderlin (Stone, 2012). And if the quality of being *natural* is connected with *good*—as it often is—this leads to a 'seemingly unhelpful implication that we human beings neither can nor should attempt to prevent this crisis' (Stone, 2012, p. 55).

---

23 'Cosmos' is an analytical category for phenomena not bound to Earth.

Everything earthbound is natural.

Leaving the analysis here, however, would challenge the very foundation of the degrowth movement (namely the call to reduce matter-energy throughput) as also the state of high entropy would also be natural. It is also questionable whether the quality of being *natural* holds any normative power. After all, as Hume ([1738–1740] 2003) remarked, *is* does not imply *ought*, and Moore postulated ([1903] 2004) that it is fallacious to explain *good* reductively, in terms of its natural qualities. While the normative appeals to the natural may lack a logical structure and do not suffice for deriving an ethical argument (Bedke, 2009; Väyrynen, 2009), it is interesting to think where the grounds for such claims arrive from if not from *nature*. Based on this chapter's definition of *nature*, ethics (as human doings) is also earthbound and, hence, always natural. For humans, there simply is no place outside nature.

The reasoning in studies critical of normative naturalism, or naturalism in general, is based on a premise of humans (and their cultures) being ontologically separate from nature. In his work, Haila (2000) showed how '[s]uch metaphysical foundationalism can be efficiently challenged by analyzing concretely how human activity and natural processes merge together.' The boundary is indeed very blurry, as revealed by Latour ([1991] 1993) and Haraway (2016). But this neither implies that there are no differences between entities of humans and nature (absolutist *ontological* enmeshing) or that nature and culture would no longer be meaningful analytical categories (absolutist *epistemological* enmeshing), nor does it indicate that everything in nature is equally 'good' (absolutist *axiological* enmeshing). Being in nature does not have to be limited to an either–or set-up.

This in-betweenness is a foundational premise for the chapter's analysis of human alienation or estrangement from nature while in nature. Whether or not humans are becoming more distant from nature, it can be at least said that the organization of human activities (i.e. how humans relate to themselves, other earthbound beings, and to their environment) has considerably changed since the very gradual exosomatic turn (Georgescu-Roegen, 1975). And if a more precise point in time is warranted, both the Agricultural and Industrial Revolution can be considered to hallmark the ecospheric crisis, the Anthropocene (Gowdy and Krall, 2013; Head, 2016; Heikkurinen, 2017b). But are humans, as a consequence of the above-mentioned developments (which signify greater environmental impact), more alienated and/or estranged from nature today?

34. Distance

This chapter adopts the term *distance* to describe the degree of human alienation and estrangement from nature. The definition departs from the Marxist tradition, which considers alienation and estrangement as undesired changes in a set of relations focusing on questions of labour and production (cf. Tolman, 1981; Vogel, 1988; Salleh, 1997). The conceptualization of distance in this chapter includes these qualitative changes in human–nature relations but also the amount of separation. That is, for Marx alienation was not a gap between humans and nature (as he considered humans to be part of nature), but first and foremost, a violated relation. However, *distance* in this chapter includes both the qualitative and the quantitative aspects of alienation and estrangement. While this chapter does not use numbers, it will attempt to quantify distance in the sense of aiming to also express the extent of it.

The proponents of degrowth (and the environmental social scientists at large) trace the distancing causes back to capitalism (Foster, 2011; Ruuska, 2017), colonialization (Thomson, 2011), development (Escobar, 2015; Demaria and Kothari, 2017), patriarchy (Dengler and Seebacher, 2019; Perkins, 2019), productivism (Latouche, [2007] 2009; Heikkurinen et al., 2019a), religion (White, 1967), and technology (Heikkurinen, 2018; Heikkurinen, 2019). In addition to these causes resulting in different kinds of distance to nature (quality), humans and their cultures are considered to be more or less distant to nature (quantity). In this book, the main culprits for the ecospheric crisis are considered diverse, and consequently, all of the above are recognized as feasible explanations for both the on-going havoc and elucidating the emergence of the claimed separation of humans from nature.

While the call to reduce matter-energy throughput is broadly shared within the degrowth movement, there seems to be hesitation about the use of the concept of nature. In fact, very few studies in the field employ the term *nature* to construct an argument for degrowth. Within the degrowth movement, there is also influence from constructivist theorists who often renounce the idea of humans becoming distant from nature (cf. Soper, 1995) and hence also disregard the rather common lay experience of alienation and estrangement. To consider the grounds for this position, the contested proposition of human alienation and estrangement must be analysed in more detail.

35. Anthropocentrism (agential)

In the spirit of degrowth, there are two obvious problems with the proposition 'humans are becoming distant from nature'. First of all, it can be considered to be anthropocentric as humans are treated as a single agent (Heikkurinen et al., 2019b). This is so-called agential anthropocentrism (ibid). That is, an analysis of contextual variables is problematically missing (Haraway, 2015; Altvater et al., 2016; Bauer, 2016; Moore, 2016). The proposition reads as if all humans were equally distant from nature. This is undoubtedly the case as there are cultural differences in human individuals, organizations, and societies. However, while it is a fair critique to say that humankind is not *the* agent in the history of the Earth, it must be accepted that humankind can be investigated as *an* agent, *a* force of nature (Heikkurinen, 2017b). If the species unit of analysis is rejected in absolute terms, then the findings of natural sciences where humans are analysed as a variable must altogether be abandoned. This is a rather absurd demand.

36. Culturalist versus naturalist

The proposition does lack cultural sensitivity.[24] In addition to this, which can be called the *culturalist critique* against the proposition, there is another, perhaps even more serious reason to contest it. The following questions shed light on the so-called naturalist critique. How can humans become distant from nature if they are embedded in it? In more generic terms, how can something be separate from something it is a part of? In other words, if humans are a product or part of nature, how could they ever be alienated or estranged from nature? Even though this naturalist critique may be sensibly rational, is it reasonable? That is, how troublesome are the political implications of this critique? How can one determine at normative implications in and from nature without assuming that *natural* implies *good* or *is* implies *ought*? And lastly, if all human doings are 'of nature,' how can there be anything unnatural or less in line with nature?

37. Nihilism

An easy way of out of this set of problems would be to abandon the concept of nature and any normative relevance of something being more of less natural. There are of course both proponents and antagonists of the concept within environmental philosophy and sociology. In this respect, degrowth theorizing can also be divided into those who employ the term *nature* and those who refrain from employing it. A decision, however, should not be rushed and hastily accepted as it may have serious repercussions for the movement. Without the term *nature*, would not the movement still need another term to describe the earthbound whole? In what context is, if not that of nature, that of spaceship Earth is the increased matter-energy flow a problem? If there is no term for the

---

24 As a conceptual investigation, this chapter does not employ the full force of the culturalist critique. There is of course great variety within cultures. Some individuals and organizations have very different perception of nature. In US culture, for example, oil executives and pagan priestesses, for instance, can have very different relationships to nature, even though they are part of the same culture of the US.

earthbound whole, how else can one derive claims about truth, beauty, and virtue beyond mere subjective preference? Is the loss of the word *nature* even prone to leading to existential nihilism?

After all, as Storey put it (2011, p. 6), 'nihilism is a problem about humanity's relation to nature, [...] the erosion of a hierarchically ordered nature in which humans have a proper place.' Leaving the concept of nature (or similar concepts) behind also means excluding the possibility of an absolute; how then is the degrowth movement expected to go about making normative arguments? Or if the concept of nature is to remain in the degrowth discourse, how could the movement respond to and overcome the respectable culturalist and naturalist critiques? Before giving my verdict, this chapter will explore the possibility of sticking with the concept of nature.

In addition to avoiding prejudice and discrimination towards the concept, it must be noted that *nature* is used in the everyday language of many and is a rather inter-subjective, shared experience among many. To test this, one can go out onto the street and ask people to show one some nature that is nearby, and several people will without hesitation point towards the closest parks, forests, waterfronts, mountains, animals, etc. It is peculiar, and perhaps paradoxical, that nature is conceptually so vague but in experience it is somewhat clear to humans what it means and where to find it.

38. Language

Thus, instead of overlooking people's experiences of nature, could not this paradox be taken as a sign of the insufficiency of human language for grasping complex phenomena? Such a stance would not yet mean that attempts to grasp complex phenomena would be in vain. It certainly remains worthwhile to continue reaching for more accurate and relevant linguistic descriptions of these multifaceted human perceptions. Acknowledging limitations is not about giving up on the task. The limitation perhaps revealed here is that human language may not be capable of capturing human experience, that is, the experience itself might always remain richer and more intense.

Despite the limitations and political risks involved, the next chapter will now try to outline a response to the critique of the use of the concept of nature. Introducing a supplement to the conceptualization of nature will hopefully succeed in this. At its simplest, the proposal of the chapter is that nature has a *core* in addition to its complex set of relations. If openness to revealing a core of nature is granted, then it will be conceivable to claim that humans are becoming distant to nature while in nature. This denotes that a slight modification in the proposal is necessary. The book will hence next advance by proposing that humans are becoming distant from *the core of nature*.

CHAPTER SIX
The core of nature

This chapter claims that nature has a core. I will elaborate this concept by looking at the core of nature using three temporal lenses: lenses of the past, future, and the present. I also claim that because forward-looking and romantic views of nature are often over-represented, for the sake of diversity and balance, we should emphasize present nature. Accordingly, the core of nature is found here and now, in the moment.

39. Disalienation

The 'a core' supplement to the conceptualization of nature can explain how humans can simultaneously be both embedded in nature yet experience increased distance from nature or alienation and estrangement from nature. Human distancing is not from nature but from the core of nature. It is the core that can become more distant to the human experience. But this conceptual innovation only solves the naturalist critique of the concept of nature. To address the other major problem, namely the culturalist critique (see issues 35–36), this chapter proceeds to amend the proposition further.

Owing to the important anthropological and sociological influences on the degrowth movement, the contextual matters are increasingly recognized as major tenet of its theory (see, e.g. the special issue on 'Geographies of Degrowth' in the journal *Environment and Planning E: Nature and Space*), and hence, it is not meaningful to merely discuss humans (the *anthropos*) as an agent in the history of nature. Therefore, to mirror these advancements, the proposal should be rephrased as follows:

Certain *human cultures* are becoming more distant to the core of nature than others. And conversely, certain human cultures are not becoming as distant to the core of nature as others are. Moreover, in order to be sensitive also to the past it could be proposed that certain human cultures are not only becoming distant to the core of nature but also *are more distant* and *have been more distant* than others.

And again, this proposal could also be deduced conversely as well. But the big question, namely what this core of nature is, is a trickier one. Similar to Heidegger's understanding of being, the core of nature unfolds gradually and it is hence largely non-representational. After all, once a representation is given after a perception, the world has already changed. This means that every attempt to represent nature misses it partly, but not fully. Something more informative, however, must and can be said about nature.

40. Temporality

Let us set the scene by considering Whitehead's seminal remark on the concept of nature, made one hundred years ago in the Tarner Lectures delivered in Trinity College:

> The explanation of nature which I urge as an alternative ideal to this accidental view of nature, is that nothing in nature could be what it is except as an ingredient in nature as it is. The whole which is present for discrimination is posited in sense-awareness as necessary for the discriminated parts. An isolated event is not an event, because every event is a factor in a larger whole and is significant of that whole. There can be no time apart from space; and no space apart from time; and no space and no time apart from the passage of the events of nature. The isolation of an entity in thought, when we think

of it as a bare 'it,' has no counterpart in any corresponding isolation in nature. Such isolation is merely part of the procedure of intellectual knowledge. (Whitehead, [1919] 2005, p. 91)

Corresponding to Whitehead's ([1919] 2005) processual conceptualization of nature, the core of nature can also be defined as a process. Whitehead (ibid, p. 36) noted: 'As in the case of everything directly exhibited in sense-awareness, there can be no explanation of this [processual] characteristic of nature.' All that can be done is to use language which may speculatively demonstrate it, and also to express the relation of this factor in nature to other factors.' And this is what we will attempt to do next: to exhibit a processual view on human–nature relations. This conceptual framing will be based on three different temporal lenses that were brought to the fore by the advanced proposal. That is, the 'becoming distant' has a future orientation; the 'are distant' has an orientation to the present, and the 'have been distant' has an orientation in the past. Consequently, I will conceptualize the core of nature through these three, classic temporal lenses: the past, future, and present.

41. Romanticism

The first lens provides a view on the core of nature as 'the past'. It reflects perhaps the most conventional understanding of nature, which is often connected with terms like *organic*, *wild*, and *pristine*. The core of nature is hence considered to be very un(human)touched nature. It is obvious that in the past, simply due to their numbers and the scale of organized economic activity, humans intervened less in the laws of nature and had a lesser impact on it. Thus, when viewed through this lens, the core of nature appears as something the Earth *had* before the gradually increasing human dominance. In other words, the core of nature is in the history of the planet.

American conservationists, such as Emerson (1836), Thoreau (1854), and Muir (1911), largely represented nature in this light.

Also, in the seminal book *The End of Nature*, McKibben (1989, p. 68) stated: '[...] we have ended the thing that has, at least in modern times, defined nature for us.' Thus, when degrowth scholars and activists influenced by the conservationist thought refer to *nature*, they often mean non-human nature or the rest of nature. It is the distinction between humans and nature that the Earth is losing as everything has become increasingly human. Consequently, the core of nature is considered to be something that is gradually disappearing from the reach of human experience, as there is less and less organic, wild, and pristine nature.

A conceptualization of the core of nature according to this view would undoubtedly receive harsh critique for representing romantic ideals. Both modernists and post-modernists reject the pre-modern longing for the time before industrialization and global human impact. For many critics it is exactly the romantic ideal of nature, something valuable in the past, that is at the heart of the ecological crisis (e.g. Morton, 2007). The practical implications for the degrowth movement that follows from applying this lens would be 'to roll back technological development' and 'return to nature', which are arguably difficult, if not impossible, to achieve.

42. Postmodernism

The second, increasingly popular lens provides a view of the core of nature as 'the future'. Nature is seen as something that humanity is heading towards. This lens is forward-looking, reflecting the progressive and optimist ambitions within the degrowth movement. One example of this kind of perspective is manifested by the Next Nature Network (2018, p. 1), an 'international network for anyone interested to join the debate on our future – in which nature and technology are fusing'. In contrast to the first lens, the 'core of nature as the future' is not extremely critical towards science and technology.

The proponents of (what is called) 'next nature' note that 'we're so surrounded by technology that it's becoming our next nature. It may sound abstract, but it's closer than you think; cars will drive themselves and heart valves are 3D printed' (ibid, p. 1). Latour ([1991] 1993) and Haraway (2016) could also be considered to represent this group of scholars and activists that seek to go forward to or toward nature by blurring the boundaries between humans and nature (Malm, 2018). Moreover, this lens also manifests in accelerationist ideas (see, e.g. Bastani, 2019), which are less about rethinking human relations with nature and more about transforming them in line with state-of-the-art techno-science.

An explanation on the core of nature derived from this post-modernist (rather than pre-modernist) view would posit that the core is something to come. It is something that humans, and why not other beings as well, can approach. Owing to the contemporary techno-capitalist hegemony, this view is perhaps attractive to many instead of the call to return back to the land. Be that as it may, the main problem with considering that humanity is moving towards the core of nature is the lack of analysis regarding the matter-energetic limits (Georgescu-Roegen, 1975; Heikkurinen, 2018) and the mainly anthropocentric care for non-humans (McShane, 2007; Heikkurinen et al., 2016).

43. Metamodern

Adopting the first, pre-modernist lens or the second, post-modernist understandings of nature, the core of nature would be something in the past or something waiting for humans in the future. But as in the classic three-fold category of time, there is also the lens of the present in addition to those of the past and future. Hence, one more understanding of the core of nature is to be disclosed conceptually, namely *the core of nature as the present*. That is, there is not only the 'old nature' and 'next nature', but also 'this nature'. This understanding of the core of nature goes beyond the pre-modernist and post-modernist views and could hence be called *meta-modern*. Conceptually speaking, the lens of the present lies in between the past and the future. It is the gift that humans have and share: this moment.

Whitehead ([1919] 2005, p. 38) used the term *moment* to mean 'all nature at an instant', which comes close to the idea of the core. A moment has no 'temporal extension, and is in this respect to be contrasted with a duration which has such extension' (ibid, p. 38). In other words, 'A moment is a limit to which we approach as we confine attention to durations of minimum extension' (ibid, p. 38). Thus, perhaps in terms of descriptive relevance about the core of nature, the lens of the present takes primacy as the other two are temporal projections—one to the past and the other to the future.

To describe the third lens further, it can be noted that it is neither optimistic (i.e. hopeful, and confident about the future) nor pessimistic (i.e. tending to see the worst aspect of things or believe that the worst will happen) as it is 'about now' rather than 'tomorrow' or the days to follow. It has its view steadily rooted in current affairs. However, a paradoxical problem with this kind of 'momentism' or 'presentism' is its lack of projection of (or even rejection of) the past and future, which is needed for managing everyday life and designing political change. Thus, in the spirit of inclusion and synthesis, the most complete understanding of the core of nature (out of these three) would include all three of these temporal lenses.

44. Process

All three viewpoints regarding the core of nature can be viewed as processes. What makes them unique and complementary is their temporal orientation and their implications for the degrowth movement that is seeking to understand human–nature relations. From the perspective of the *core of nature as past*, human–nature relationships are processes of humans becoming distant to the core of nature. It is a story of alienation and estrangement from the nature of the past. And when the culturalist critique is also integrated in this lens, the following, core-of-nature (CON) premise can be formulated:

Certain human cultures are and have been nearer to the core of nature and are becoming nearer to the core of nature than others.

In other words, according to this premise, some cultures are and have been 'less developed' than others, and hence closer to the core of nature. This premise would also implicitly suggest that the undesired process of certain human cultures becoming distant to the core of nature could be reverted by learning from the primitive, indigenous cultures that have not techno-scientifically developed at a similar pace than the rest of the world (see, e.g. Thomson, 2011; Demmer and Hymmel, 2017). And even if seen as a very niche phenomenon, becoming nearer to the core of nature is happening (e.g. in the back-to-the-land movement). From the point of view of matter-energy throughput, the premise has a strong case as in the past significantly less matter-energy travelled through human cultures.

According to the view of *core of nature as future*, again, the human–nature relationship is about moving towards a new, more desired state. Through this lens, it seems that the process of approaching the core of nature could be supported by having openness to innovation and by amalgamating the boundaries between humans and non-human nature (see, e.g. Likavčan and Scholz-Wäckerle, 2018). After all, in the future, nature will be increasingly cyborgian or hybrid-like (at least until the collapse, one could argue). The CON premise can hence also be supported from this lens: certain human cultures are and have been nearer to the core of nature and are becoming nearer to the core of nature than others. The benchmark, though, is the future rather than the past.

Another way of putting this would be to say that certain cultures are lagging behind in terms of approaching the core of nature. This 'futuristic' proposition is an antonym of the 'past-istic' proposition of pastism. Hence, the CON premise can develop into very different kinds of normative claims. The first could claim that humans need to slow down and connect with the kind of nature that the Earth had in the past, while the second could call for acceleration and connecting with the new opportunities emerging. On the one hand, these two lenses can be perceived as opponents, but on the other hand, they can also be considered to be complementary, or even mutually opposing so they cancel each other out. This leads us to considering the insights that can be gained from the premise in relation to the third lens.

Viewing the *core of nature as present* indicates that the process of human–nature relations is not about moving backwards or forward but balancing between the two. It considers the human–nature relationship as an oscillation between the past and the future, a sort of a balancing act, where equilibrium is the core of nature. The lens does not convey the ancient ideas that Botkin (1990) referred to under the banner, 'the balance of nature' but is more aligned with dynamic ideas of equilibrium, where nature is always changing. Nature is a process, according to Whitehead ([1919] 2005), into which humans, in the vocabulary of Heidegger ([1927] 2012), are thrown (*geworfen*). I hereby combine and extend these works by saying that humans are not only thrown in the world— as Heidegger phrased it—but also in the process of nature—as Whitehead remarked. Humans and other earthbound beings are thrown into nature, where we learn to be. The inquiry henceforth is about *being-in-nature*.

The process encourages humans to develop skills for coping if they want to stay alive. While the human place in nature is defined by this constant balancing, at times, human cultures in nature are further from the core of nature, the equilibrium, than others. On the global scale, the Anthropocene would be an example of this imbalance or asymmetry in the current human–nature relationship, where human cultures (some more than others) have become very powerful and created an asymmetry that is harmful for the diversity of earthbound existence. Here it is also important to note that some human cultures can be more out of balance than others, and hence, further away from the dynamic equilibrium, a state of balance between continuing processes.

CHAPTER SIX

45. Presentism

This chapter has investigated human–nature relations in the light of the recent call for degrowth and outlined a culturally-sensitive response to a (conceived) paradox where humans embedded in nature experience alienation and estrangement from it. This book holds that human cultures in nature can be, as well as become, more distant to nature if nature is assumed to have a core. We are being alienated in nature. In other words, if nature has a core, then grounds for understanding the experienced distance emerge. Certain human cultures certainly are and have been nearer to the core of nature and are becoming nearer to the core of nature than others. The yardstick for the distance can be viewed through the lenses of 'the past', 'the future', and 'the present'.

I posit that while the degrowth movement should be inclusive of all temporal perspectives, the lens of the present should be emphasized in order to balance out the prevailing romanticism and futurism, in particular, in the theory and practice of degrowth. The core of nature is an equilibrium. This view on human–nature relations forms a philosophical foundation for the politics of degrowth that should not be about having less matter-energy throughput for the sake of less matter-energy throughput but to slow down the rate of human-induced metabolism so that Earth could come closer to a point of balance, enabling the continuity of diverse existence. A normative implication of this chapter for the degrowth movement could be phrased as follows: *emphasize the present.*

In other words, the implications for the degrowth movement would be to neither accept the romantic nor the futuristic ideals of human–nature relations but to have an emphasis on the present, the existing situation. Rather than *aiming to balance*, this implies *balancing*. And as the processes of nature are currently so disturbed by human cultural growth, the ever-increasing use of resources and amounts of waste that extend beyond the absorptive capacity of the ecosphere, a way to move closer to the equilibrium would only happen through radically reducing the flow of matter-energy throughput. This is the process of degrowing.

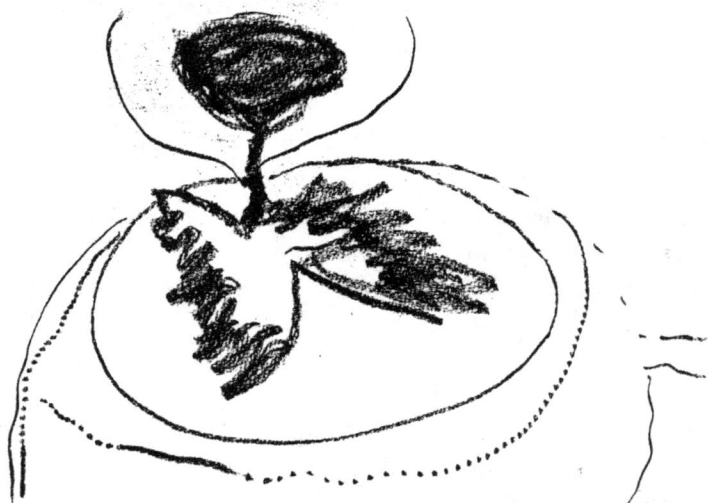

CHAPTER SEVEN
Implications

This chapter outlines five implications for the degrowth movement. First, we in the movement should keep it real by holding on to a realist notion of truth while engaging in inter-subjective action. Second, the understanding of culture–nature metabolism should be the base of the movement's intellectual endeavours and guide action. Third, the idea that a good life for everyone, all the time, everywhere is possible should be abandoned. It creates inertia by placing too strict criteria on the movement's initiatives. Fourth, it is not enough to trust positivist science on limits; we must experience the finitude of being, and hereby advance limit realization (e.g. on what should not be done). Fifth, we need openness to cosmic phenomena (that is not limited to technological practices).

46. Stay real

It goes without saying that many of us—those who identify with the degrowth movement—talk about *degrowth* without offering the term much elaboration. The reason for this is, I think, that we share an experience of what degrowth is. That is, in order for us to make sense of the discourses of degrowth, we must somewhat be in the same world, which again is in nature.

Our lifeworlds are overlapping or have a degree of inter-subjectivity in nature. Without this similarity in what is experienced, sharing our thoughts (about degrowth, for example) would be extremely difficult, if not impossible. This basic epistemological assumption, of course, is not limited to the degrowth movement, but applies more generally to phenomena. A phenomenon, like degrowth, is real (at minimum) in the sense that it is shared in experience. And the more inter-subjectively the phenomenon is experienced, the more real it is. Let us call this 'the proof of the real'. It is not, however, completely democratic. What I mean by this is that by one million people sharing the experience of 'the necessity to grow' and one person experiencing its negation, 'the necessity to degrow', does not make the preceding experience more real.

The real is something one cannot calculate or quantify because it is inherently qualitative. Qualities are always contextual and contingent, among other things, on time and place. Depending on our encounters, changes in quality occur and vary. For example, once a calculation is finished (let us say it takes 10 seconds), the qualities of the object under calculation have already altered. It is not only the place and its cultural variance that changes us, but also time itself. We mature, we compost. This reasoning is of course indebted to Heraclitus' attempts to step on the same stream twice.

But then again, we also have another interesting pre-Socratic philosopher, Parmenides, who claimed that being is eternal. Instead of seeing constant change and dynamism in the world, he was a proponent of inertia and stasis forming the nature of the cosmos. Arguably, it is here that the still on-going realism–anti-realism quarrel and the mono- and polytheism dispute have their origins.

For me, both of these views are reductions of the world. The nature of the cosmos is neither in constant change nor eternal. The world is not one, neither is it many. In a way, we could say it is both, but I think a more precise formulation would be to say that it is neither and that it falls *between change and inertia*. It is between one and the many. To reiterate this, the world (including we who live in it) is neither static nor dynamic but a process, which includes, or even requires, oscillation between movement and stasis, and concerns unity and difference. It has a beginning, a journey, and an end (or beginnings, journeys, and endings).

A process is that which can embrace the realms of finitude and infinity without being confined to either one. It hereby includes experiences along this continuum, and beyond. We may feel more or less finite, but never completely limited. We know that we die, but we do not know what death is. The process I here refer to is real to the extent it inter-subjectively corresponds with the nature of the cosmos.

To come back to our context, or case, the degrowth movement, we must ask: What do we mean when we say *degrowth*? This is an onto-epistemological question concerning the degree of inter-subjectivity of the phenomenon being considered. To what extent are we talking about the same phenomenon?

I am glad to see that the degrowth movement is gaining attention in mainstream media and policies etcetera but I think there are reasons to be sceptical about the sphere of the shared. In other words, how real is degrowth or to what extent is degrowth real?

47. Understand metabolism

Degrowth thinking has many intellectual roots, one of them stretching back to Romanian ecological economist, Georgescu-Roegen (1906–1994) and his magnum opus *The Entropy Law and the Economic Process* (1971). The ideas of his opus were developed by Daly (1938–2022), whose works many of us may know better. Degrowth theorizing arising from these two economists is pretty straightforward in the sense that what *degrowth* refers to is first and foremost the reduction of matter-energy throughput or the metabolic flow from human action. I have called this the minimalist definition of *degrowth* (Heikkurinen, 2019; see Chapter 4 in this book) as it seems to me that it sets the lowest requirement for what can be considered degrowth.

If we follow this minimalist definition of degrowth (i.e. degrowth as the reduction of matter-energy throughput) then we must always ask to what extent and *how* certain initiatives reduce or slow down the metabolic flow.

The movement has come far from the foundations of the concept of degrowth. How many of us are talking about the minimalist definition of degrowth? Not very many. So, what is degrowth then? Degrowth seems to be an idea, a principle, a strategy, and a practice. It is a movement, a conference, a journal. It is people, a planet, care. It is about the Global North and Global South. Degrowth is a communist slogan, ecosocialism, a climate case, a means for decolonialization, posthumanism, a feminist way to be in the world. If you say that degrowth is all these for you, then you are approaching a maximalist definition of *degrowth*. While multiplicity, pluralism, and intersectionality are of course important cultural phenomena that should be hosted within the movement, the struggles should be conjoined to the minimalist definition of the movement. The increasing matter-energy throughput is the main struggle of the degrowth movement. The maximalist definition of *degrowth* may also be linked to failure to create effective change. The set of causes simply becomes too massive for anyone to handle, perhaps becoming too over-whelming and even a source of anxiety and depression.

48. Reject over-inclusivity

The above-mentioned definition of *degrowth*, 'degrowth to the max', is vague and fuzzy. It is actually a non-definition due its over-inclusivity. It contains a tendency to aspire to providing a good life for everyone, all the time, everywhere, which I will coin here as 'The GLATE discourse[25]'. It gives a smooth, ethical appearance and a cool progressive vibe. But it may fail to deliver the badly needed reorganization of our affairs in a way that would actually reduce matter-energy throughput and finally enable the continuity of diverse earthbound being.

The political claim of the book is that the degrowth movement

---

25 The term GLATE is an acronym of my choice but interestingly, as a general word, it also has another meaning and origin. *Glate* (*glāte̽*) comes from Vulgar Latin *glacia*, from Latin *glacies*, presumably referring to ice. This is quite fitting, as the GLATE discourse is arguably metaphorically freezing the movement.

should reject the GLATE discourse on two bases. First of all, the GLATE discourse legitimizes the continuity of the growing human sphere as the proposed changes—for example, voluntary simplicity and self-provisioning—are not executed due to their seeming failure to contribute to providing a good life for everyone, all the time, everywhere. So, the standard for what can be counted as proper degrowth action is set so high and made so ambitious that nothing is actually sufficient or good enough. And consequently, it seems that the current growing state of affairs is preferred and continues to prevail.

Second, the GLATE discourse should be rejected on onto-epistemological grounds. We will simply never have the understanding of what is a good life for everyone, all the time, everywhere. In other words, there is a problem of knowing, which is quite like the challenges that grand planning economies have faced. Anarchism provides a valuable lesson on the importance of decentralized governance and also surfaces an epistemological critique of such hubris. The solution is to find means of supporting participation on a local scale rather than snooping to brains of the great minds of our time, not to mention obeying the powerful, centralized states. At its simplest, which body would know what GLATE is and how to provide it? The EU? The UN? The IPCC? China? Sweden? Andreas Malm? Georgios Kallis? Julia Steinberger?

The (more) ontological side of the problem is that the call for degrowth in line with the GLATE discourse does not connect to being. Owing to its global scale, the GLATE discourse relies on techno-science in its attempts to demarcate the limits of growth. They are something like 1.5 Celsius, 350 ppm, 2000 tons of CO_2 equivalent, and so on. How real or effective are these calculations of limits? Well, obviously not very. Instead, they are quite arbitrary and silly as they do not comment on the manner in which reorganization is to be conducted. They are not only positivistic but also overlook the complexities of our will-to-transform and will-to-growth.

49. Experience limits

It is not numbers, letters, or symbols (not even the snail!) that connect our lifeworlds in the degrowth movement—but it is the experience of limits. The inter-subjective experience, that we need to degrow, is the central qualitive difference to other movements out there and the thing that unites us. It all basically boils down to the lowest common denominator, the minimalist definition of *degrowth* (as the reduction of matter-energy throughput), not the GLATE discourse where everyone can add as much as possible.

To avoid building a movement without meaningful and feasible direction, I suggest that whenever we talk about degrowth, we should specify what we mean by *degrowth*. What is it for you in addition to the minimalist definition? To me, degrowth is the experience of finitude, degrowing. And once this is taken care of, we can begin practicing limits.

This is of key importance, not only for the above-mentioned reasons but particularly because of the fact that without an experience of finitude (i.e. what is considered enough and what the limits are deemed to be) we are left at the vagaries of the worldwide techno-capitalist elites.

50. Get cosmic

Also, the degrowth movement is finite. It is earthbound. It is not only 'bound' to the Earth in the sense of coming from the Earth, but it also largely treats issues related to the earth. Moreover, the main motivation of the movement is based on the idea of nature's limits. We claim that there is a need for economic and population degrowth (in terms of matter-energy throughput) in order to enable the continuity of diverse life on Earth, in order to enable sustainability.

The claim that life on a finite planet simply cannot handle infinite growth in the number of people and their affluence is today empirically well supported. Also, the bottom-up strategies and top-down policies for reaching degrowth are often discussed within the movement. But the question that needs to be addressed is the not limited to the Earth, or life on Earth; it is also about the cosmos.

The degrowth movement does not have explicated cosmologies but different stances towards the cosmos could be identified in the literature on degrowth. The relationship between the Earth and its environment, space, remains an underexplored territory in the degrowth movement, in particular in academia. The reasons for this can only be speculated about, but it is understandable that the cosmos is foreign to many degrowthers due to its perceived distance and assumed irrelevance to earthbound affairs.

However, such a strict division and experience of separateness between the Earth and its environment may be fallacious and inconsistent with degrowth theory. Indeed, it would be naïve to posit that the cosmos is without any influence on Earth and vice versa. The other extreme of the degrowth movement on this issue seems equally mistaken. Perhaps the implied possibilities of techno-science and dreams of building colonies outside this planet are even more dangerous in regard to securing diverse life on Earth.

Hitherto, the degrowth movement has not needed a cosmology, but later on, it may be something worth considering. Many of the first-tier strategies and policies for reducing the growth of human numbers and affluence can be executed without engaging in cosmic experiences. However, as the movement matures, it must position itself not only in relation to the Earth and its beings, it must also explore its place within cosmos.

That is, even if there is no dire need for a cosmology of degrowth, I call for a 'cosmic turn'. Engaging in discussions on the cosmos can be fruitful for advancing the theory on degrowth by outlining a more holistic (self-)understanding of the phenomenon as different cosmologies offer varying justifications for strengthening the case for degrowth. Since cosmos is also claimed to be intricately connected to the absence and revival of meaning (in the claimed secular age, dominated by techno-capitalism), the inclusion of cosmic experiences in the movement can also contribute to cultural cohesion and the on-going identity work of the movement.

Conclusion

The expansion of human cultures around the globe has signified an anomaly in the recorded history of the planet. A single species has become a global force. It transforms—or perhaps we can talk about we transforming biotic and abiotic entities at an unprecedented pace, creating amounts and kinds of waste never seen before. An example of these wastes are anthropogenic greenhouse emissions, such as carbon dioxide and methane, which reach new records every year (WMO, 2018). These residues of development have created changes in the ecosphere (and continue to do so), including the climate, which have led to a notable reduction in Earth's biodiversity that is, now even jeopardizing the existence of humankind (Swanson, 1995; McKinney and Lockwood, 1999; Ceballos et al., 2015).

This is the big picture—the major, scientifically broadly accepted causes and consequences of the ecospheric crisis: the Technological Revolution. But what can be done about this growth of human cultures' impact in nature? The conventional response from the hegemonic techno-capitalist system is something along the lines that:

> We need more growth so that we can take care of the planet. The problems increased affluence and population create will be solved by means of technology. There is no need to worry. What we need is hope.

Many people in the movement are of course sceptical towards this kind of rhetoric about infinite growth. We are aware of the harm done by the mounting human affluence and numbers, particularly in the Global North but also in many communities and families in the so-called Global South. And we also comprehend that a technological solution is unable to fix a cultural problem.

The fact that the degrowth movement is operating translocally is a prominent harbinger of growth-critical voices and forms an important platform and institutional support for many initiatives against growth. But like most cultural activity, the scholarship and activism of degrowth—self-sufficiency and self-provisional initiatives excluded—are dependent on economic growth. This problem area is widely acknowledged, and solutions are being reconnoitred. The movement, however, is also highly contingent on advanced technology and scientific knowledge, which are not only products of growth culture but are also speeding up the metabolism.

How to break free from the growth culture of techno-capitalism? This book concludes that the degrowth movement, including its scholarship, should pay more attention to the experience of degrowth, which is about being finite. It simply is not enough to engage in some activities here and there, to 'do degrowth', if one then returns to growth culture. *Being degrowth* and *degrowth being* are more than practices. They are beyond thoughts and discourses. They refer to the whole manner in which the movement is in the world. They direct us to the lifeworld of degrowthers. We must metamorphose into degrowth with our souls and cells, as well as let go of the idea that growth is needed in some sectors of society. Growth is not necessary. We do not even need spiritual or moral growth, but we shall let go of the whole idea of growth for some time now. If we do, then we might become sober enough to stop. And once we stop, we should wait. And once we have waited, surprises will happen. This unknown can help us to see what are the things that could be allowed to spread, but not grow. But let us not try to calculate that. Let us welcome scaling out, not upscaling.

It is not enough to change our language, activities, or structures.

Emphasis ought to be placed on *being*. Growth culture cannot be challenged by merely gaining control of the means of production or appropriating means for better ends. The growth imperative runs so deep in our cultural fabric that it is the way we are in the world. To counter the increasing matter-energy throughput, the degrowth movement must refrain from highly technological practices, as well as avoid fetishizing low tech. The ontic does not suffice. Every step down in the degree of technology is surely supportive of slowing down the human–nature metabolism: this is the minimalist definition of *degrowth*. Of course, our being in the world cannot be reduced to thermodynamic applications. We are not here to just reduce, reuse, and recycle. That is the make-believe function of the eco-modernist machine.

Our inherent will-to-transform cannot be directed to degrowth as it distracts us from the existential question. The move from the growth mode of being to one of degrowth requires a metamorphosis *in being*. It is fundamental, nothing gradual, and it results in a completely different type of *lifeworld*, to use a phenomenological term from Husserl. It is not only a new ethic and new form of politics, it is also another aesthetic. What we perceive to be good and beautiful in the new degrowth mode of being is built on the experience of finitude, a deep (embodied) understanding that everything has limits. Even this idea is limited and will die.

Degrowth as the experience of being finite also unfolds a unique spatio-temporality, which is about the present time-space. We are now in the right place, at the right time. But it is also about deep geological time-space where human life feels quite insignificant. We are a lost culture. But as we degrow, we are no longer paralysed by sadness or driven by the anger related to the destroyed world. Neither are we expecting the world to become something beautiful and good. We dwell degrowth.

***

The distilled argument of the book is that *degrowth is about the experience of being finite*. Also, the movement is very limited and far from being omnipotent. Paying more attention to our mode of being lets us realize the lessons and intricacies of our limited being. Inspired by Emmanuel Severino's ([1982] 2016) *The Essence of Nihilism*, this is non-transcendental and anti-metaphysical in the sense that there is no 'non-being', a sphere where things would come into being. Instead, the argument on the experience the limits is immanent, or possibly in limbo between transcendence and immanence, 'trammanent'.

In this book, I have argued that limits should not be imposed on us by natural scientists or policymakers; they should be something that we should collectively consider and define as caring beings. And for us to be able to collectively deliberate, discuss, and determine the limits, we must experience finitude in being. I encourage everyone to explore limits in diverse situations with precaution, as well as to experiment with limits together. It is equally the responsibility of the movement to set limits on its members as it is up to the members to find the limits. No one can know their limits without getting feedback from their surroundings. In his book *Steps to an Ecology of Mind*, Gregory Bateson (1972) showed us that this is how culture systems emerge; they depend upon feedback loops to control balance. Once practices based on inter-subjective knowing of the limits begins to emerge, mastery will be achieved eventually. And importantly for the degrowth movement's ambition to reduce contingency on growth, this shared experience of limits helps us to reduce our dependency on the resource-hungry and wasteful practices of techno-capitalism. We will hereby also establish independency from the misuses of power in regard to the human and more-than-human lifeworlds.

References

Abram, D. (1996). *The Spell of the Sensuous*. Pantheon Books, New York.

Ahern, L. (2001). Language and agency. *Annual Review of Anthropology*, 20, 109–137.

Alcott, B. (2005). Jevons' paradox. *Ecological Economics*, 54(1), 9–21.

Alexander, S. (2013). Voluntary simplicity and the social reconstruction of law: Degrowth from the grassroots up. *Environmental Values*, 22(2), 287-308.

Arendt, H. ([1971] 1978). *The Life of the Mind: The Groundbreaking Investigation on How We Think*. A Harvest Book, San Diego.

Asara, V., Otero, I., Demaria, F., & Corbera, E. (2015). Socially sustainable degrowth as a social–ecological transformation: Repoliticizing sustainability. *Sustainability Science*, 10(3), 375–384.

Aydin, C. (2007). Nietzsche on Reality as Will to Power: Toward an "Organization–Struggle" Model. *The Journal of Nietzsche Studies*, 33(1), 25–48.

Bannon, B.E. (2014). *From Mastery to Mystery: A Phenomenological Foundation for an Environmental Ethic*. Ohio University Press, Athens.

Barad, K. (2014). Posthumanist performativity: Toward an understanding of how matter comes to matter. *Signs*, 40(1), 801–831.

Barnosky, A.D., Hadly, E.A., Bascompte, J., Berlow, E.L., Brown, J.H., Fortelius, M., Getz, W.M., Harte, J., Hastings, A., Marquet, P.A., Martinez, N.D., Mooers, A., Roopnarine, P., Vermeij, G., Williams, G.W., Gillespie, R., Kitzes, J., Marshall, C., Matzke, N., Mindell, D.P., Revilla, E., & Smith, A.B. (2012). Approaching a state shift in Earth's biosphere. *Nature*, 486(7401), 52–58.

Barnosky, A.D., Matzke, N., Tomiya, S., Wogan, G.O.U., Swartz, B., Quental, T.B., Marshall, C., McGuire, J.L., Lindsey, E.L., Maguire, K.C., Mersey, B., & Ferrer, E.A. (2011). Has the Earth's sixth mass extinction already arrived? *Nature* 471, 51–57.

Bastani, A. (2019). *Fully Automated Luxury Ccommunism*. Verso Books, London.

Bateson, G. (1972). *Steps to an Ecology of Mind: Collected Essays in Anthropology, Psychiatry, Evolution, and Epistemology*. University of Chicago Press, Chicago.

Bauer, A.M. (2016). Questioning the Anthropocene and its silences: Socioenvironmental history and the climate crisis. *Resilience: A Journal of the Environmental Humanities*, 3, 403–426.

Baykan, B.G. (2007). From limits to growth to degrowth within French green politics. *Environmental Politics*, 16(3), 513–517.

Bedke, M.S. (2012). Against normative naturalism. *Australasian Journal of Philosophy*, 90, 111–129.

Bennett, J. (2004). The force of things steps toward an ecology of matter. *Political Theory*, 32(3), 347–372.

Bennett, J. (2010). *Vibrant Matter – A Political Ecology of Things*. Duke University Press, Durham.

Binswanger, M. (2001). Technological progress and sustainable development: What about the rebound effect? *Ecological Economics*, 36(1), 119–132.

Biro, A. (2005). *Denaturalizing Ecological Politics: Alienation from Nature from Rousseau to the Frankfurt School and Beyond*. University of Toronto Press, Toronto.

Blok, V. (2011). Establishing the truth: Heidegger's reflections on gestalt. *Heidegger Studies*, 27, 101–118.

Blok, V. (2017). *Ernst Jünger's Philosophy of Technology: Heidegger and the Poetics of the Anthropocene*. Routledge, New York.

Blok, V. (2018). Contesting the will: Phenomenological reflections on four structural moments in the concept of willing. *Journal of the British Society for Phenomenology*, 49(1), 18–35

BNEF (Bloomberg New Energy Finance) (2015). *Global Trends in Clean Energy Investment – Rebound in Clean Energy Investment in 2014 Beats Expectations* (Mills, L., presenter), 9 January.

Boltanski, L., & Chiapello, E. ([1999] 2005). *The New Spirit of Capitalism*. (Elliott, G., trans.). Verso, New York.

Bonaiuti, M. (ed.) (2011). *From Bioeconomics to Degrowth: Georgescu-Roegen's 'New Economics' in Eight Essays*. Routledge, London.

Bonnedahl, K.J., & Heikkurinen, P. (eds.) (2019). *Strongly Sustainable Societies: Organising Human Activities on a Hot and Full Earth*. Routledge, London.

Bonnedahl, K.J., Heikkurinen, P., & Paavola, J. (2022). Strongly sustainable development goals: Overcoming distances constraining responsible action. *Environmental Science & Policy*, 129, 150–158.

Bookchin, M. (1962). *Our Synthetic Environment* (Herber, L., pseudon.). Knopf, New York.

Botkin, D.B. (1990). *Discordant Harmonies: A New Ecology for the Twenty-First Century*. Oxford University Press, New York.

Boulding, K.E. (1966). The economics of the coming spaceship earth. In Jarrett, H. (ed.), *Environmental Quality in a Growing Economy* (pp. 3–14). Johns Hopkins University Press, Baltimore.

Bourdieu, P. ([1972] 1977). *Outline of a Theory of Practice* (Nice, R., transl.). Cambridge University Press, Cambridge.

Bourdieu, P. (1986). The Forms of Capital. (Nice, R., transl.). In Richardson, J.E. (ed.), *Handbook of Theory of Research for the Sociology of Education* (pp. 241–58). Greenwood Press, Westport.

Brand, U. (2016). 'Transformation' as a new critical orthodoxy: The strategic use of the term 'transformation' does not prevent multiple crises. *GAIA-Ecological Perspectives for Science and Society*, 25(1), 23–27.

Brown, C.S., & Toadvine, T. (eds.) (2012). *Eco-phenomenology: Back to the Earth Itself*. SUNY Press, New York.

Brown, K., O'Neill, S., & Fabricius, C. (2013). Social science understandings of transformation. In International Social Science Council (ed.), *World Social Science Report 2013: Changing Global Environments* (pp. 100–106). Publishing and Unesco Publishing, Paris.

Carlile, P.R., Nicolini, D., Langley, A., Tsoukas, H. (2013). How matter matters: objects, artifacts and materiality in organization studies. In Carlile, P.R., Langley, A. (eds.), *How Matter Matters: Objects, Artifacts, and Materiality in Organization Studies*, (pp. 1–31). Oxford University Press, Oxford.

Cattaneo, C., D'Alisa, G., Kallis, G., & Zografos, C. (2012). Degrowth futures and democracy. *Futures*, 44(6), 515–523.

Ceballos, G., Ehrlich, P.R., Barnosky, A.D., García, A., Pringle, R.M., & Palmer, T.M. (2015). Accelerated modern human–induced species losses: Entering the sixth mass extinction. *Science Advances*, 1(5), e1400253.

Chancel, L., & Piketty, T. (2015) *Carbon and Inequality: From Kyoto to Paris Trends in the Global Inequality of Carbon Emissions (1998–2013) & Prospects for an Equitable Adaptation Fund.* Available at: http://piketty.pse.ens.fr/files/ChancelPiketty2015.pdf.

Collard, R.C., Harris, L.M., Heynen, N., & Mehta, L. (2018). The antinomies of nature and space. *Environment and Planning E: Nature and Space*, 1(1–2), 3–24.

Cook, J., Oreskes, N., Doran, P.T., Anderegg, W.R., Verheggen, B., Maibach, E.W., Carlton, J.S., Lewandowsky, S., Skuce, A.G., Green, S.A., Nuccitelli, D., Jacobs, P., Richardson, M., Winkler, B., Painting, R., & Rice, K. (2016). Consensus on consensus: A synthesis of consensus estimates on human-caused global warming. *Environmental Research Letters*, 11(4), 048002.

Cosme, I., Santos, R., & O'Neill, D.W (2017) Assessing the degrowth discourse: A review and analysis of academic degrowth policy proposals. *Journal of Cleaner Production*, 149, 321–334.

D'Alisa, G., Demaria, F., & Kallis, G. (eds.) (2015). *Degrowth: A Vocabulary for a New Era.* Routledge, Oxon.

Dahlstrom D.O. (2013). *The Heidegger Dictionary.* Bloomsbury, London.

Dalle Pezze, B. (2006). Heidegger on Gelassenheit. *Minerva – An Internet Journal of Philosophy*, 10, 94–122.

Daly, H.E. (1990). Sustainable growth: An Impossibility Theorem. *Development* 3/4, 45–47.

Daly, H.E. (1979). Entropy, growth and the political economy of scarcity. In Smith, V.K. (ed.), *Scarcity and Growth Reconsidered* (pp. 67–94). John Hopkins University Press, Baltimore.

Daly, H.E. (1992). *Steady-State Economics.* Earthscan, London.

Daly, H.E (1996). *Beyond Growth: The Economics of Sustainable Development.* Beacon Press, Boston.

Daly, H.E. (2005). Economics in a full world. *Scientific American*, 293(3), 100–107.

Davis, B.W. (2007). *Heidegger and the Will: On the Way to Gelassenheit.* Northwestern University Press, Illinois.

de Freitas, L.C., & Kaneko, S. (2011). Decomposing the decoupling of CO_2 emissions and economic growth in Brazil. *Ecological Economics*, 70(8), 1459–1469.

Demaria, F., & Kothari, A. (2017). The Post-Development Dictionary agenda: Paths to the pluriverse. *Third World Quarterly*, 38(12), 2588–2599.

Demaria, F., Schneider, F., Sekulova, F., & Martinez-Alier, J. (2013). What is degrowth? From an activist slogan to a social movement. *Environmental Values*, 22(2), 191–215.

Demmer, U., & Hummel, A. (2017). Degrowth, anthropology, and activist research: the ontological politics of science. *Journal of Political Ecology*, 24(1), 610–622.

Dengler, C., & Seebacher, L.M. (2019). What about the global south? Towards a feminist decolonial degrowth approach. *Ecological Economics*, 157, 246–252.

Di Pippo, A.F. (2000). The concept of poiesis in Heidegger's An Introduction to Metaphysics. In Shikiar, D. (ed.), *Thinking Fundamentals* (pp. 1–33). Institute for Human Science, Vienna.

Dickens, P. (1997). Local environments, the division of labour and alienation from nature. *Local Environment*, 2(1), 83-87.

Dietz, R., O'Neill, D. (2013). *Enough Is Enough: Building a Sustainable Economy in a World of Finite Resources*. Routledge, Oxon.

Dietz, T., & Rosa, E.A. (1997). Effects of population and affluence on CO2 emissions. *Proceedings of the National Academy of Sciences*, 94(1), 175–179.

Drengson, A.R. (1995). *The Practice of Technology: Exploring Technology, Ecophilosophy, and Spiritual Disciplines for Vital Links*. SUNY Press, New York.

Duncan, R.C. (1993). The life-expectancy of industrial civilization: The decline to global equilibrium. *Population and Environment*, 14, 325–357.

EC (European Commission) (2015). *EU Action on Climate*. Available at: http://ec.europa.eu/clima/policies/brief/eu/.

Ehrenfeld, D. (1978). *The Arrogance of Humanism*. Oxford University Press, New York.

Elhacham, E., Ben-Uri, L., Grozovski, J., Bar-On, Y.M., & Milo, R. (2020). Global human-made mass exceeds all living biomass. *Nature*, 588(7838), 442–444.

Ellis, E.C. (2011). Anthropogenic transformation of the terrestrial biosphere. *Philosophical Transactions of the Royal Society A: Mathematical, Physical and Engineering Sciences*, 369(1938), 1010–1035.

Ellis, E.C., Klein Goldewijk, K., Siebert, S., Lightman, D., & Ramankutty, N. (2010). Anthropogenic transformation of the biomes, 1700 to 2000. *Global Ecology and Biogeography*, 19(5), 589–606.

Ellul, J. ([1954] 1973). *The Technological Society* (Wilkinson, J., transl.). Vintage Books, New York.

Emerson, R.W. (1836). *Nature*. James Munroe and Company, Boston.

Emirbayer, M., & Mische, A. (1998). What is agency? *American Journal of Sociology*, 103(4), 962–1023.

Escobar, A. (2015). Degrowth, postdevelopment, and transitions: A preliminary conversation. *Sustainability Science*, 10(3), 451-462.

Evans, D. (2005). A risk of total collapse: We would be foolish to take for granted the permanence of our fragile global civilisation. *The Guardian*, 21 December.

Figueiredo, L., Krauss, J., Steffan-Dewenter, I., & Sarmento Cabral, J. (2019). Understanding extinction debts: Spatio–temporal scales, mechanisms and a roadmap for future research. *Ecography*, 42(12), 1973-1990.

Finnveden, G. (2000). On the limitations of life cycle assessment and environmental systems analysis tools in general. *International Journal of Life Cycle Assessment*, 5(4), 229–238.

Foster, J.B. (2000). Marx's ecology: Materialism and Nature. *Monthly Review Press*, New York.

Foster, J.B. (2011). Capitalism and degrowth: An impossibility theorem. *Monthly Review*, 62(8), 26–33.

GEN (Global Ecovillage Network), (2024). *Our Work*. Available at: https://ecovillage.org/our-work/.

Georgescu-Roegen, N. ([1970] 2011). The Entropy Law and the Economic Problem. In Bonaiuti, M. (ed.), *From Bioeconomics to Degrowth: Georgescu-Roegen's 'New Economics' in Eight Essays* (pp. 49–57). Routledge, London.

Georgescu-Roegen, N. (1971). *The Entropy Law and the Economic Process*. Harvard University Press, Cambridge.

Georgescu-Roegen, N. (1975). Energy and economic myths. *Southern Economic Journal*, 41(3), 347–381.

Giddens, A. (1984). *The Constitution of Society: Outline of the Theory of Structuration*. Polity Press, Cambridge.

Goodland, R., & Daly, H. (1996). Environmental sustainability: Universal and non-negotiable. *Ecological Applications*, 6(4), 1002–1017.

Gowdy, J., & Krall, L. (2013). The ultrasocial origin of the Anthropocene. *Ecological Economics*, 95, 137–147.

Haila, Y. (2000). Beyond the nature-culture dualism. *Biology and Philosophy*, 15(2), 155–175.

Hailwood, S. (2015). *Alienation and Nature in Environmental Philosophy*. Cambridge University Press, Cambridge.

Hamilton, C. (2013). *Earthmasters: The Dawn of the Age of Climate Engineering*. Yale University Press, New Haven.

Hamilton, C (2016). The theodicy of the "Good Anthropocene". *Environmental Humanities*, 7(1), 233–238.

Haraway, D. (2015). Anthropocene, capitalocene, plantationocene, chthulucene: Making kin. *Environmental Humanities*, 6(1), 159–165.

Haraway, D. (2016). *Staying with the Trouble: Making Kin in the Chthulucene*. Duke University Press, Durham.

Harman, G. (2009). *Prince of networks: Bruno Latour and Metaphysics*. re.press, Prahran.

Head, L. (2016). *Hope and Grief in the Anthropocene: Re-conceptualising Human–Nature Relations*. Routledge, London.

Heidegger, M. ([1927] 2012). *Being and Time* (Macqarrie, J., & Robinson, E., trans.). Blackwell Publishing, Malden.

Heidegger, M. ([1936–1944] 2006). *Mindfulness* (Emad, P., & Kalary, T., transl.). Continuum, London.

Heidegger, M. ([1944] 2010). *Country Path Conversations* (Davis, B.W., transl.). Indiana University Press Bloomington, Indianapolis.

Heidegger, M. ([1952–1962] 1977). *The Question Concerning Technology and Other Essays* (Lovitt, W., transl.). Garland Publishing, New York.

Heidegger, M. ([1959] 1966). *Discourse on Thinking: A Translation of Gelassenheit* (Anderson, J.M., & Freund, E.H., transl.). Harper & Row, New York.

Heidegger, M. ([1959] 2001). *Poetry, Language, Thought* (Hofstadter, A., transl.). HarperCollins, New York.

Heidegger, M. ([1976] 1981). "Only a God Can Save Us": The Spiegel Interview (1966) (Richardson, W., transl.), In Sheehan, T. (ed.), *Heidegger – The Man and the Thinker* (pp. 45–67). Transaction Publishers, New Brunswick.

Heikkerö, T. ([2012] 2014). *Ethics in Technology: A Philosophical Study*. Lexington Books, Lanham.

Heikkurinen, P. (2017a). The relevance of von Wright's humanism to contemporary ecological thought. *Acta Philosophica Fennica*, 93, 449–463.

Heikkurinen, P. (ed.) (2017b). *Sustainability and Peaceful Coexistence for the Anthropocene*. Routledge, Oxon.

Heikkurinen, P. (2018). Degrowth by means of technology? A treatise for an ethos of releasement. *Journal of Cleaner Production*, 197, 1654–1665.

Heikkurinen, P. (2019). Degrowth: A metamorphosis in being. *Environment and Planning E: Nature and Space*, 2(3), 528–547.

Heikkurinen, P. (2021). The nature of degrowth: Theorising the core of nature for the degrowth movement. *Environmental Values*, 30(3), 367–385.

Heikkurinen, P. (2023). Throughput. In Haddad, B.M., & Solomon, B.D. (eds.), *Dictionary of Ecological Economics: Terms of the New Millennium* (pp. 545–546). Edward Elgar Publishing, Cheltenham.

Heikkurinen, P., & Hohenthal, J. (2024). Sustaining local practices: Introductory remarks. *Acta Borealia*, 41(1), 1–6.

Heikkurinen, P., Rinkinen, J., Järvensivu, T., Wilén, K., & Ruuska, T. (2016). Organising in the Anthropocene: An ontological outline for ecocentric theorising. *Journal of Cleaner Production*, 113, 705–714.

Heikkurinen, P., Ruuska, T., Kuokkanen, A., & Russell, S. (2019a). Leaving productivism behind: Towards a holistic and processual philosophy of ecological management. *Philosophy of Management*, 20, 21–36.

Heikkurinen, P., Ruuska, T., Wilén, K., & Ulvila, M. (2019b). The Anthropocene exit: Reconciling discursive tensions on the new geological epoch. *Ecological Economics*, 164, 106–369.

Hickel, J., & Kallis, G. (2020). Is green growth possible? *New Political Economy*, 25(4), 469–486.

Hoekstra, J.M., Boucher, T.M., Ricketts, T.H., & Roberts, C. (2005). Confronting a biome crisis: global disparities of habitat loss and protection. *Ecology Letters*, 8(1), 23–29.

Holland, A. (1997). Substitutability: Or, why strong sustainability is weak and aburdly strong sustainability is not absurd. In Foster, J. (ed.), *Valuing Nature? Ethics, Economics and the Environment* (pp. 119–134). Routledge, London.

Hornborg, A. (2014). Ecological economics, marxism, and technological progress: some explorations of the conceptual foundations of theories of ecologically unequal exchange. *Ecological Economics*, 105, 11–18.

Hume, D. ([1738–1740] 2003). *A Treatise of Human Nature*. Dover, New York.

Illich, I. ([1973] 2009). *Tools for Conviviality*. Marion Boyars Publishers, London.

Introna, L.D. (2009). Ethics and the speaking of things. *Theory, Culture & Society,* 26(4), 25–46.

Introna, L.D. (2015). Algorithms, governance, and governmentality on governing academic writing. *Science, Technology and Human Values,* 41(1), 17–49.

IPCC (Intergovernmental Panel on Climate Change) (2013). *Climate Change 2013: The Physical Science Basis.* Cambridge University Press, New York.

IPCC (Intergovernmental Panel on Climate Change) (2014). *Fifth Assessment Report.* Available at: http://www.ipcc.ch/report/ar5/.

IPCC (Intergovernmental Panel on Climate Change) (2023). *Sixth Assessment Report.* Available at: https://www.ipcc.ch/report/ar6/syr/.

Jackson, T. (2009). *Prosperity Without Growth: Economics for a Finite Planet.* Earthscan, Oxon.

Jänicke, M. (2008). Ecological modernisation: New perspectives. *Journal of Cleaner Production,* 16(5), 557–565.

Johnson, J. (1988). Mixing humans and nonhumans together: The sociology of a door-closer. *Social Problems,* 35(3), 298–310.

Jones, C. (2016). The world of finance. *diacritics,* 44(3), 30–54.

Joubert, K., & Dregger, L. (2015). *Ecovillage – 1001 Ways to Heal the Planet.* Triarchy Press, Devon.

Kallis, G. (2011). In defence of degrowth. *Ecological Economics,* 70(5), 873–880.

Kallis, G., Demaria, F., & D'Alisa, G. (2015). Introduction: Degrowth. In D'Alisa, G., Demaria, F., & Kallis, G. (eds.), *Degrowth: A Vocabulary for a New Era* (pp. 1–17). Routledge, London.

Kallis, G., Kerschner, C., & Martinez-Alier, J. (2012). The economics of degrowth. *Ecological Economics,* 84, 172–180.

Kerschner, C. (2010). Economic de-growth vs. steady-state economy. *Journal of Cleaner Production,* 18(6), 544–551.

Ketola, T. (2010). Five leaps to corporate sustainability through a corporate responsibility portfolio matrix. *Corporate Social Responsibility and Environmental Management,* 17(6), 320–336.

Knappett, C., & Malafouris, L. (2008). Material and nonhuman agency: An introduction. In Knappett, C., Malafouris, L. (eds.), *Material Agency: Towards a Non-anthropocentric Approach* (pp. ix–xix). Springer, New York.

Küpers, W. (2016). Phenomenology of embodied and artful design for creative and sustainable inter-practicing in organisations. *Journal of Cleaner Production.* 135, 1436–1445.

Latouche, S. ([2007] 2009). *Farewell to Growth* (Macey, D., transl.). Polity Press, Cambridge.

Latour, B. ([1999] 2009). *Politics of Nature* (Porter, C., transl.). Harvard University Press, Boston.

Latour, B. ([1991] 1993). *We Have Never Been Modern.* Harvard University Press, Cambridge.

Lazzarato, M. (2015). Neoliberalism, the Financial Crisis and the End of the Liberal State. *Theory, Culture & Society,* 32(7–8), 67–83.

LeVasseur, T., & Warren, L. (2019). Redesigning community as an ecovillage: Lessons from Earthaven. In Bonnedahl, K., & Heikkurinen, P. (eds.), *Strongly Sustainable Societies: Organising Human Activities on a Hot and Full Earth.* Routledge, London.

Li, T.M. (2007). *The Will to Improve: Governmentality, Development, and the Practice of Politics.* Duke University Press, Durham.

Liao, Z., Peng, S., & Chen, Y. (2022). Half-millennium evidence suggests that extinction debts of global vertebrates started in the Second Industrial Revolution. *Communications Biology,* 5(1311), 1–8.

Likavčan, L., & Scholz-Wäckerle, M. (2018). Technology appropriation in a degrowing economy. *Journal of Cleaner Production,* 197, 1666–1675.

Lockie, S. (2004). Collective agency, non-human causality and environmental social movements: A case study of the Australian 'Landcare Movement'. *Journal of Sociology,* 40(1), 41–57.

Lorek, S., & Spangenberg, J.H. (2014). Sustainable consumption within a sustainable economy – Beyond green growth and green economies. *Journal of Cleaner Production,* 63, 33–44.

MacIntyre, A. (1981). *After Virtue.* University of Notre Dame Press, Notre Dame.

MacIntyre, A. (1999). Social structures and their threats to moral agency. *Philosophy,* 74(3), 311–329.

Malm, A. (2016). *Fossil Capital: The Rise of Steam Power and the Roots of Global Warming*. Verso Books, New York.

Martínez-Alier, J. (2009). Socially sustainable de-growth. *Development and Change*, 40(6), 1099–1119.

Martínez-Alier, J., Pascual, U., Vivien, F.D., & Zaccai, E. (2010). Sustainable degrowth: Mapping the context, criticisms and future prospects of an emergent paradigm. *Ecological Economics*, 69(9), 1741–1747.

Max-Neef, M. (1991). *Human Scale Development: Conception, Application and Further Reflections*. The Apex Press, New York.

McKibben, B. (1989). *The End of Nature*. Random House, London.

McKinney, M.L., & Lockwood, J.L. (1999). Biotic homogenization: a few winners replacing many losers in the next mass extinction. *Trends in Ecology & Evolution*, 14(11), 450–453.

McShane, K. (2007). Anthropocentrism vs. nonanthropocentrism: Why should we care? *Environmental Values*, 16(2), 169–185.

Meadows, D.H., Meadows, D.H., Randers, J., & Behrens III, W.W. (1972). *The Limits to Growth: A Report to the Club of Rome's Project on the Predicament of Mankind*. Universe Books, New York.

Meagher, R. (1988). Techne. *Perspecta*, 24, 159–164.

Mol, A.P., & Sonnenfeld, D.A. (2000). Ecological modernisation around the world: An introduction. *Environmental Politics*, 9(1), 1–14.

Mol, A.P., & Spaargaren, G. (2000). Ecological modernisation theory in debate: A review. *Environmental Politics*, 9(1), 17–49.

Moore, G.E. ([1903] 2004). *Principia Ethica*. Dover, New York.

Moore, J.W. (2016). (ed.). *Anthropocene or Capitalocene? Nature, History, and the Crisis of Capitalism*. PM Press, Oakland.

Morton, T. (2007). *Ecology Without Nature: Rethinking Environmental Aesthetics*. Harvard University Press, Cambridge

Muir, J. (1911). *My First Summer in the Sierra*. Houghton Mifflin, Boston.

Murphy, R. (1995). Sociology as if nature did not matter: An ecological critique. *British Journal of Sociology*, 46(4), 688–707.

Mylan, J. (2015). Understanding the diffusion of sustainable product-service systems: insights from the sociology of consumption and practice theory. *Journal of Cleaner Production*, 97, 13–20.

Næss A. ([1974] 1989). *Ecology, Community and Lifestyle: Outline of an Ecosophy* (Rothenberg, D., ed. & transl.). Cambridge University Press, Cambridge.

Næss, A. (1987). Self-realization: An ecological approach to being in the world. *The Trumpeter*, 4(3), 35–41.

Næss, P., & Høyer, K.G. (2009). The emperor's green clothes: Growth, decoupling, and capitalism. *Capitalism Nature Socialism*, 20(3), 74–95.

Nancy, J.L. ([1996] 2000). *Being Singular Plural* (Richardson, R.D., & O'Byrne A.E., transl.). Stanford University Press, Stanford.

Next Nature Network (2018). *About.* Available at: https://www.nextnature.net/about/.

Nietzsche, F. ([1882] 2001). *The Gay Science: With a Prelude in German Rhymes and an Appendix of Songs* (Williams, B., ed., Nauckhoff, J., transl.). Cambridge University Press, Cambridge.

Nietzsche, F. ([1883–1891] 1997). *Thus Spake Zarathustra* (Common, T., transl.). Wordsworth, London.

Nietzsche, F. ([1883–1888] 1968). *The Will to Power* (Kaufmann, W., & Hollingdale, R.J., transl.). Random House, New York.

O'Neill, J., Holland, A., & Light, A. (2008). *Environmental Values*. Routledge, London.

Oberle, B., Bringezu, S., Hatfield-Dodds, S., Hellweg, S., Schandl, H., Clement, J., and Cabernard, L., Che, N., Chen, D., Droz-Georget, H., Ekins, P., Fischer-Kowalski, M., Flörke, M., Frank, S., Froemelt, A., Geschke, A., Haupt, M., Havlik, P., Hüfner, R., Lenzen, M., Lieber, M., Liu, B., Lu, Y., Lutter, S., Mehr, J., Miatto, A., Newth, D., Oberschelp, C., Obersteiner, M., Pfister, S., Piccoli, E., Schaldach, R., Schüngel, J., Sonderegger, T., Sudheshwar, A., Tanikawa, H., van der Voet, E., Walker, C., West, J., Wang, Z., & Zhu, B. (2019). *Global Resources Outlook 2019: Natural Resources for the Future We Want*. A Report of the International Resource Panel. United Nations Environment Programme, Nairobi.

Oxfam (2015). *Extreme Carbon Inequality: Why the Paris Climate Deal Must put the Poorest, lowest Emitting and Most Vulnerable people first*. Available at: www.oxfam.org/sites/www.oxfam.org/files/file_attachments/mb-extreme-carbon-inequality-021215-en.pdf.

Parkes, G. (2003). Lao, Zhuang and Heidegger on nature and technology. *Journal of Chinese Philosophy*, 30(1), 19–38.

Parrique, T., Barth, J., Briens, F., Kerschner, C., Kraus-Polk, A., Kuokkanen, A., & Spangenberg, J.H. (2019). *Decoupling Debunked: Evidence and Arguments Against Green Growth as a Sole Strategy for Sustainability.* European Environmental Bureau, Deurne.

Pauly, D. (2014). Homo sapiens: Cancer or parasite? *Ethics in Science and Environmental Politics,* 14(1), 7–10.

Perkins, P.E.E. (2019). Climate justice, commons, and degrowth. *Ecological Economics,* 160, 183–190.

Piketty, T. ([2013] 2014). *Capital in the Twenty-first Century* (Goldhammer, A., transl.). Cambridge, London.

Plumwood, V. (2001). Nature as agency and the prospects for a progressive naturalism. *Capitalism Nature Socialism,* 12(4), 3–32.

Polanyi, K. ([1994] 2001). *The Great Transformation.* Beacon Press, Boston.

Porter, J.I. (2006). Nietzsche's theory of the will to power. In Ansell Pearson, K. (ed.), *A Companion to Nietzsche* (pp. 548–564). Blackwell Publishing, Malden.

Reckwitz, A. (2002). Toward a theory of social practices: a development in culturalist theorizing. *European Journal of Social Theory,* 5(2), 243–263.

Rentmeester, C. (2016). *Heidegger and the Environment.* Rowman & Littlefield, London.

Richardson, K., Steffen, W., Lucht, W., Bendtsen, J., Cornell, S.E., Donges, J.F., Drüke, M., Fetzer, I., Bala, G., von Bloh, W., Feulner, G., Fiedler, S., Gerten, D., Gleeson, T., Hofmann, M., Huiskamp, W., Kummu, M., Mohan, C., Nogués-Bravo, D., Petri, S., Porkka, M., Rahmstorf, S., Schaphoff, S., Thonicke, K., Tobian, A., Virkki, V., Wang-Erlandsson, L., Weber, L., & Rockström, J. (2023). Earth beyond six of nine planetary boundaries. *Science Advances,* 9(37), eadh245.

Rinkinen, J. (2013). Electricity blackouts and hybrid systems of provision: Users and the 'reflective practice'. *Energy, Sustainability and Society,* 3(1), 25.

Rinkinen, J., Jalas, M., & Shove, E. (2015). Object-relations in accounts of everyday life. *Sociology,* 49(5), 870–885.

Ritchie, P.D., Clarke, J.J., Cox, P.M., & Huntingford, C. (2021). Overshooting tipping point thresholds in a changing climate. *Nature,* 592(7855), 517–523.

Rockström, J., Steffen, W., Noone, N., Persson, Å., Chapin III, S.F., Lambin, E.F., Lenton, T.M., Scheffer, M., Folke, C., Schellnhuber, H.J., Nykvist, B., de Wit, C.A., Hughes, T., van der Leeuw, S., Rodhe, H., Sörlin, S., Snyder, P.K., Costanza, R., Svedin, U., Falkenmark, M., Karlberg, L., Corell, R.W., Fabry, V.J., Hansen, J., Walker, B., Liverman, D., Richardson, K., Crutzen, P., & Foley, J.A. (2009). A safe operating space for humanity. *Nature*, 461, 472–475.

Røpke, I. (2009). Theories of practiced: New inspiration for ecological economic studies on consumption. *Ecological Economics*, 68(10), 2490–2497.

Ruuska, T. (2017). Capitalism and the absolute contradiction in the Anthropocene. In Heikkurinen, P. (ed.), *Sustainability and Peaceful Coexistence for the Anthropocene* (pp. 51–67). Routledge, Oxon.

Saito, K. (2023). *Marx in the Anthropocene: Towards the Idea of Degrowth Communism*. Cambridge University Press, Cambridge.

Salleh, A. (1997). *Ecofeminism as Politics. Nature, Marx and the Postmodern*. Zed Books, London.

Samerski, S. (2018). Tools for degrowth? Ivan Illich's critique of technology revisited. *Journal of Cleaner Production*, 197, 1637–1646.

Schaffartzik, A., Mayer, A., Gingrich, S., Eisenmenger, N., Loy, C., & Krausmann, F. (2014). The global metabolic transition: Regional patterns and trends of global material flows, 1950–2010. *Global Environmental Change*, 26, 87–97.

Schatzki, T.R. (2007). Introduction. *Human Affairs: Postdisciplinary Humanities & Social Sciences Quarterly*, 17(2), 97–100.

Schatzki, T.R. (2002). *Site of the Social: A Philosophical Account of the Constitution of Social Life and Change*. Penn State Press, University Park.

Schatzki, T.R. (2014). Practices, governance and sustainability. In Strengers, Y., Maller, C. (eds.), *Social Practices, Intervention and Sustainability: Beyond Behaviour Change* (pp. 15–30). Routledge, Oxon.

Schneider, F., Kallis, G., & Martinez-Alier, J. (2010). Crisis or opportunity? Economic degrowth for social equity and ecological sustainability. Introduction to this special issue. *Journal of Cleaner Production*, 18(6), 511–518.

Schwinn, T. (2008). Individual and collective agency. In Turner, S.P., & Outwhite, W. (eds.), *The Sage Handbook of Social Science Methodology* (pp. 302–315). Sage, London.

Scott, J.C. (1998). *Seeing like a State: How Certain Schemes to Improve the Human Condition Have Failed*. Yale University Press, Yale.

Sekulova, F., Kallis, G., Rodríguez-Labajos, B., & Schneider, F. (2013). Degrowth: from theory to practice. *Journal of Cleaner Production*, 38, 1–6.

Severino, E. ([1982] 2016). *The Essence of Nihilism* (Donis G., transl.). Verso, London.

Shove, E., Pantzar, M., & Watson, M. (2012). *The Dynamics of Social Practice: Everyday Life and How it Changes*. Sage, London.

Soper, K. (1995). *What Is Nature? Culture, Politics and the Nonhuman*. Wiley-Blackwell, Oxford.

Steffen, W., Richardson, K., Rockström, J., Cornell, S.E., Fetzer, I., Bennett, E.M., Biggs, R., Carpenter, S.R., de Vries, W., de Wit, C.A., Folke, C., Gerten, D., Heinke, H., Mace, G.M., Persson, L.M., Ramanthan, V., Reyers, B., & Sörlin, S. (2015). Planetary boundaries: Guiding human development on a changing planet. *Science*, 347(6223), 1259855.

Stone, A. (2012). Hölderlin and human-nature relations. In Brady, E., & Phemister, P. (eds.), *Human-Environment Relations: Transformative Values in Theory and Practice* (pp. 55–67). Springer, Dordrecht.

Storey, D. (2011). Nihilism, Nature, and the Collapse of the Cosmos. *Cosmos and History: The Journal of Natural and Social Philosophy*, 7(2), 6–25.

Suarez-Villa, L. (2000). *Invention and the Rise of Technocapitalism*. Rowman & Littlefield, Lanham.

Suarez-Villa, L. (2009). *Technocapitalism: A Critical Perspective on Technological Innovation and Corporatism*. Temple University Press: Philadelphia.

Swanson, T. (ed.) (1995). *The Economics and Ecology of Biodiversity Decline: The Forces Driving Global Change*. Cambridge University Press, Cambridge.

Tainter, J.A (1990). *The Collapse of Complex Societies*. Cambridge University Press, Cambridge.

Tapio, P. (2005). Towards a theory of decoupling: Degrees of decoupling in the EU and the case of road traffic in Finland between 1970 and 2001. *Transport Policy*, 12(2), 137–151.

Thomson, B. (2011). Pachakuti: Indigenous perspectives, buen vivir, sumaq kawsay and degrowth. *Development*, 54(4), 448–454.

Thoreau, H.D. (1854). *Walden; or, Life in the Woods*. Ticknor and Fields, Boston.

Tolman, C. (1981). Karl Marx, alienation, and the mastery of nature. *Environmental Ethics*, 3(1), 63–74.

Tomlinson, B., Blevis, E., Nardi, B., Patterson, D.J., Silberman, M., & Pan, Y. (2013). Collapse informatics and practice: Theory, method, and design. *ACM Transactions on Computer-Human Interaction*, 20(4), 1–26

Ulvila, M. & Wilén, K. (2017). Engaging with the Plutocene: moving towards degrowth and postcapitalist futures. In Heikkurinen, P., (ed.), *Sustainability and Peaceful Coexistence for the Anthropocene* (pp. 119-139). Routledge, Oxon.

UN (United Nations) (1992). *United Nations Framework Convention on Climate Change.* United Nations, New York. Available at: https://unfccc.int/files/essential_background/background_publications_htmlpdf/application/pdf/conveng.pdf.

UN (United Nations) (2012). *The Future We Want.* Resolution (A/RES/66/288) Adopted by the General Assembly on 27 July.

UNEP (United Nations Environment Programme) (2011). *Decoupling Natural Resource Use and Environmental Impacts from Economic Growth.* A Report of the Working Group on Decoupling to the International Resource Panel. Available at: https://www.resourcepanel.org/.

Vadén, T. (2014). Next Nature and the Curse of Oil. *Next Nature*, 21 February.

Väyrynen, P. (2009). Normative appeals to the natural. *Philosophy and Phenomenological Research*, 79(2), 279–314.

Verbeek, P.-P. (2006). Materializing morality: Design ethics and technological mediation. *Science, Technology and Human Values*, 31(3), 361–380.

Victor, P.A. (2008). *Managing without Growth: Slower by Design, Not Disaster.* Edward Elgar Publishing, Cheltenham.

Vincent, S. (2008). A transmutation theory of inter-organizational exchange relations and networks: applying critical realism to analysis of collective agency. *Human Relations*, 61(6), 875–899.

Vitali, S., Glattfelder, J.B., & Battiston, S. (2011). The network of global corporate control. *PloS ONE*, 6(10), e25995.

Vogel, S. (1988). Marx and alienation from nature. *Social Theory and Practice*, 14(3), 367–387.

Vogel, S. (1999). For and against nature. *Rethinking Marxism*, 11(4), 102–112.

von Wright, G.H. (1987) *Tiede ja ihmisjärki – Suunnitusyritys.* (Leikola, A., transl.). Otava, Helsinki.

von Wright, G.H. (1978). *Humanismen som livshållning.* Månpocket, Stockholm.

WCED (World Commission on Environment and Development) (1987). *Our Common Future*. Report of the World Commission on Environment and Development. United Nations, New York.

White, L. (1967). The historical roots of our ecologic crisis. *Science*, 155(3767), 1203–1207.

Whitehead, A.N. ([1919] 2005). *The Concept of Nature*. Cambridge University Press, Cambridge.

Wiedmann, T.O., Schandl, H., Lenzen, M., Moran, D., Suh, S., West, J., Kanemoto, K. (2015). The material footprint of nations. *Proceedings of the National Academy of Sciences*, 112(20), 6271–6276.

Winner, L. (1977). *Autonomous Technology: Technics-out-of-control as a Theme in Political Thought*. MIT Press, Massachusetts.

WMO (World Meteorological Organization) (2018). *WMO Greenhouse Gas Bulletin – The State of Greenhouse Gases in the Atmosphere Based on Global Observations through 2017*. Available at: https://community.wmo.int/en/wmo-greenhouse-gas-bulletin-14.

Wright, E.O. (2013). Transforming capitalism through real utopias. *American Sociological Review*, 78(1), 1–25.

Wrigley, E.A. (2010). *Energy and the English Industrial Revolution*. Cambridge University Press, Cambridge.

Zalasiewicz, J., Williams, M., Smith, A., Barry, T.L., Coe, A.L., Bown, P.R., Brenchley, P., Cantrill, D., Gale, A., Gibbard, P., Gregory, F.J., Hounslow, M.W., Kerr, A.C., Pearson, P., Knox, R., Powell, J., Waters, C., Marshall, J., Oates, M., Rawson, P., & Stone, P. (2008). Are we now living in the Anthropocene? *GSA Today*, 18(2), 4–8.

Zhang, Z. (2000). Decoupling China's carbon emissions increase from economic growth: An economic analysis and policy implications. *World Development*, 28(4), 739–752.

Zimmerman, M.E. (1983). Toward a Heideggerean ethos for radical environmentalism. *Environmental Ethics*, 5(2), 99–131.

Zimmerman, M.E. (1994). *Contesting Earth's Future: Radical Ecology and Postmodernity*. University of California Press, Berkley.

Žižek, S. (2012). *Don't Act. Just Think* [video]. YouTube, 28 August. Available at https://www.youtube.com/watch?v=IgR6uaVqWsQ.

Index

A

abiotic 1, 111
acceleration 70, 99
action 11, 12, 24, 27, 29, 31, 50, 56, 57, 58, 59, 60, 64, 72, 103, 105, 107
aesthetic 9, 113
affluence 3, 4, 13, 17, 108, 109, 111, 112
agency 15, 23, 24, 25, 29, 30, 31, 32, 33, 35, 40, 42, 71, 72
agent 24, 29, 32, 53, 59, 87, 94
agential 30, 65, 87
alienation 7, 81, 84, 85, 86, 87, 93, 98, 101. See also estrangement
animal 30, 60, 63
anthro-
  anthromes 2, 40, 47, 72
  anthropocene 56, 60, 62, 70, 72, 76, 77, 86, 100
  anthropocentric 24, 36, 69, 87, 97
  anthropocentrism 36, 41, 87
  anthropogenic 1, 2, 3, 6, 47, 53, 57, 58, 64, 71, 72, 81, 111
  anthropological 93
  anthropologist 65
  anthropos 93
anti-
  anti-capitalist ix
  anti-decoupling vi, 16
anxiety 106
Arendt, Hannah 68, 69
art 21, 53, 62, 63, 64, 81, 97
artefacts 44
assemblage 24
atechnology 43, 46. See also releasement, releasers
autonomy, autonomous 11, 29, 31, 32, 39, 72
awaiting 7, 73. See also waiting
axiology, axiological 85

control 22, 29, 39, 44, 113, 114
convivial 6, 39
core of nature 7, 90, 93, 94, 95, 96, 97, 98, 99, 100, 101. See also CON
corporation, corporate 17
cosmos, cosmic, cosmology 11, 77, 104, 105, 109
craft 63
culture, cultural ix, 4, 7, 8, 10, 12, 13, 15, 24, 29, 36, 55, 77, 83, 85, 88, 103, 112, 113, 114
cumulative, cumulation 6, 28, 39, 45, 47, 56
cyborg 40

D

Daly, Herman 2, 3, 16, 17, 19, 20, 41, 55, 56, 57, 77, 105
Dasein 54
decoupling vi, 16. See also anti-decoupling
degrow 4, 104, 108, 113
degrowing 4, 101, 108
degrowth ix, x, xi, xiii, xiv, 2, 3, 4, 5, 6, 7, 8, 9, 10, 11, 12, 13, 16, 17, 18, 19, 20, 23, 25, 29, 40, 42, 43, 44, 45, 46, 47, 49, 50, 54, 55, 56, 57, 58, 59, 60, 62, 69, 70, 71, 72, 73, 74, 76, 77, 78, 81, 83, 85, 86, 87, 88, 89, 93, 96, 98, 101, 103, 104, 105, 106, 107, 108, 109, 112, 113, 114
being 78
definition of 17, 45, 105, 106, 108, 113
discourse 3, 89
mode of being 9, 113
movement ix, xi, 5, 6, 7, 8, 9, 11, 12, 13, 17, 18, 44, 54, 55, 58, 59, 69, 70, 71, 72, 73, 74, 81, 85, 87, 89, 93, 96, 98, 101, 103, 104, 105, 106, 108, 109, 112, 113, 114
ontology 54
scholars 19, 96
society 17, 18, 20, 23, 25, 43, 44, 55
theory xi, 6, 50, 109
democracy, democratic 50, 104
depression, depressive 20, 106
der Wille zur Macht 61
development 2, 15, 17, 28, 29, 35, 39, 51, 52, 83, 86, 96, 111
disalienation vii, 93
disclose, disclosing 23, 51
discourse 3, 4, 5, 7, 45, 49, 50, 51, 57, 59, 60, 63, 65, 89, 106, 107, 108
distant, distance 18, 37, 85, 86, 87, 88, 90, 93, 94, 95, 98, 99, 101
dualism 7, 57, 76
dwell 9, 35, 53, 113

E

experiential 10

F

fantasy 16
fascist, fascism 45, 46
finite ix, xi, 2, 5, 9, 10, 11, 19, 105, 108, 112, 113, 114. See also finitude
fossil ix, 2, 20, 40, 43, 56
fundamental xi, 7, 9, 28, 61, 113
future, futurist ix, 8, 24, 25, 29, 46, 52, 64, 68, 72, 74, 78, 93, 95, 96, 97, 98, 99, 100, 101

G

GDP 19, 70
Gelassenheit, gelassen 36, 37, 68, 69, 71
geography, geographer 65, 77
Georgescu-Roegen, Nicholas 6, 17, 19, 25, 39, 40, 41, 55, 60, 77, 82, 83, 86, 97, 105
gestalt 53, 54, 62
Ge-stell 22, 23, 64
GLATE 106, 107, 108
Global South 17, 106, 112
GNP 19
god 29, 72
good life 8, 11, 103, 106, 107
government 50
growth x, 1, 2, 3, 4, 6, 9, 10, 12, 13, 15, 16, 17, 19, 20, 35, 49, 52, 56, 58, 59, 61, 62, 64, 67, 69, 70, 72, 74, 75, 77, 101, 107, 108, 109, 111, 112, 113, 114
  culture of 12
  economic 16, 19, 20, 35, 49, 52, 64, 69, 70, 74, 112
  green 56
  population 1
GWP 19

H

Haraway, Donna 85, 87, 97
Harman, Graham 8
hegemony, hegemonic x, 17, 24, 64, 97, 111
Heidegger, Martin 5, 8, 18, 19, 21, 22, 23, 25, 26, 28, 29, 30, 36, 37, 39, 41, 42, 43, 44, 45, 50, 51, 54, 64, 68, 69, 71, 73, 74, 75, 76, 94, 100
Heraclitus 104
hope 13, 67, 72, 73, 111. See also optimism, optimistic
hubris, hybris ix, 10, 17, 107

of being 9
of everything 22
rejection of 11
sense of 10
testing 11
to expansion 2
understanding of 10, 11
local 1, 2, 15, 50, 55, 58, 81, 107
logos 53

M

machine 13, 19, 32, 67, 113
Marx, Karl 84, 86
material 2, 4, 11, 16, 19, 20, 24, 27, 32, 44
matter-energy 4, 5, 6, 8, 9, 10, 11, 15, 17, 19, 20, 21, 22, 28, 40, 43, 44, 45, 46,
    47, 49, 54, 55, 56, 57, 58, 59, 63, 67, 69, 70, 71, 72, 74, 76, 77, 78, 83,
    85, 87, 88, 99, 101, 105, 106, 108, 113. See also throughput
McKibben, Bill 96
meaning 61, 63, 106, 109
media 105
meditation, meditative vi, 35, 37, 38, 42, 45, 58, 73
Merleau-Ponty, Maurice 5
meta-
    metabolic 4, 8, 17, 19, 47, 55, 56, 59, 70, 77, 105
    metabolism vii, 9, 11, 68, 101, 103, 105, 112, 113. See also throughput
    metamodern vii, 97
    metamorphosis x, xi, 6, 7, 9, 52, 53, 54, 69, 70, 71, 72, 73, 75, 76, 113
    metaphysical 9, 54, 61, 85, 114
    metaphysics 73
mindful 69
minimal 17, 45, 105, 106, 108, 113. See also degrowth, definition of
mobil-
    mobility 1, 40
    mobilization 12, 64
    mobilizing 13
modernity 26, 28, 83
moment 75, 76, 93, 97, 98
moral 15, 29, 30, 32, 33, 35, 36, 112. See also ethos
more-than-human 8, 57, 114
mystery 37, 69

N

Næss, Arne 5, 16, 81
narrative 3, 56

74, 76
renewable 2, 56
resource 2, 17, 20, 22, 23, 45, 114. See also capital
reveal 22, 28
revolution 1, 3, 15, 86, 111
romantic 8, 75, 93, 96, 101

S

scarcity 20, 45
science x, 10, 13, 23, 64, 81, 96, 97, 103, 107, 109
    scientific 12, 13, 64, 71, 76, 112
    scientist 12
self-
self-provisioning 74, 107. See also subsistence
self-sufficiency 18, 112
sense x, 9, 10, 11, 19, 22, 29, 37, 40, 42, 53, 57, 71, 74, 75, 76, 86, 94, 95, 103,
        104, 105, 108, 114
Severino, Emmanuel 114
sex 59
sharing 18, 103, 104
sine qua non vi, 49. See also degrowth, definition of
situated 24, 25
situation 23, 42, 101
skill xiii, 46, 62, 83, 100
slow ix, 13, 70, 99, 101, 105
social vi, 11, 12, 13, 15, 17, 21, 23, 24, 25, 26, 27, 28, 29, 32, 35, 41, 46, 50, 51,
        55, 56, 57, 61, 63, 64, 65, 72, 77, 81, 82, 86
    change 15, 17, 23, 24, 26, 29, 32
    practice 27, 28. See also practice
society 17, 18, 20, 23, 25, 43, 44, 52, 55, 59, 76, 112
sociologist, sociology 29, 84, 88
space 3, 10, 12, 25, 75, 77, 94, 109, 113
species 1, 3, 35, 36, 39, 41, 43, 46, 59, 67, 82, 83, 87, 111
spirit 10, 50, 54, 59, 87, 98
standing reserve 32, 33, 36, 45
state 3, 32, 41, 61, 63, 76, 81, 85, 97, 99, 100, 107
stock 57
structure 12, 85
subject 29, 38, 71
subsistence 59. See also self-provisioning
sufficiency, sufficient 15, 18, 62, 74, 75, 107, 112
sustainability 3, 4, 16, 20, 108
    sustainable change xiv
    sustainable growth 56

T